God's Arrow Against Atheists
By Henry Smith
With chapters by C. Matthew McMahon

Copyright Information

God's Arrow Against Atheists, by Henry Smith with chapters by C. Matthew McMahon

Changes made to this edition do not affect the overall language of the document, nor do they change the writer's intention. Spelling, grammar, and formatting changes have been made, and modernized wording is used in specific cases to help today's reader more fully grasp the intention of the author.

© 2012 by Puritan Publications and A Puritan's Mind

Published by Puritan Publications
A Ministry of A Puritan's Mind
4101 Coral Tree Circle #214
Coconut Creek, FL 33073
www.puritanpublications.com
www.apuritansmind.com

All rights reserved. No part of this publication may be reproduced, stored in a retrieval system or transmitted in any form by any means, electronic, mechanical, photocopy, recording or otherwise, without the prior permission of the publisher, except as provided by USA copyright law.

First Electronic Edition, 2012, Second Edition 2024
First Paperback Edition, 2012, Second Edition, 2024
Manufactured in the United States of America

eISBN: 978-1-937466-67-1
ISBN: 978-1-937466-68-8

Table of Contents

Introduction to This Volume 4

Meet Henry Smith 6

CHAPTER 1: There is a God 9

CHAPTER 2: Christianity the Only True Religion 18

CHAPTER 3: Against Infidels 38

CHAPTER 4: Islam: a False Religion 72

CHAPTER 5: Roman Catholicism is the Apostate Church and Antichrist 87

CHAPTER 6: Against Schismatics 143

Other Works Published by Puritan Publications 148

Introduction to This Volume
By C. Matthew McMahon, Ph.D., Th.D.

This work by Henry Smith (1550–1591) is a *gem*. However, Henry Smith is *little* known. Smith's works are comprehensively *outstanding* (including select sermons on Janah and Nebuchadnezzar which have now been republished and modernized by Puritan Publications). He lived only a short time (dying at the age of 41, although some documentation exists showing he may have died at 51). He was a *second generation* reformer and a precursor to Puritanism. That means he did not sit in the company of Luther, Calvin or Zwingli, since he lived a short time *after* they died, but he also did not live during the time of the more well-known Puritans and the Westminster Assembly (c. 1620–1680). Instead, he fills a gap in his lifetime of rubbing shoulders with the *fathers* of puritanism (men like William Perkins (1558–1602), William Ames (1576–1633) and Thomas Cartwright (1535–1603), as well as his mentor Richard Greenham (1535–1594)).[1] In his day he was known as a powerful preacher – the "prime preacher of the nation".

This particular book was one of Smith's most popular works, and went through dozens of editions and reprints during his lifetime (his sermons in general had gone through *eighty-five* editions by 1620). *God's Arrow* focuses on utterly destroying paganism (the atheism of

---

[1] Puritan Publications has published the first volume of Richard Greenham's *works* now available.

the natural man), Islam (the religion of carnality) and Roman Catholicism (the religion of the deceived, apostate and Antichristian establishment posing as God's authority in the world), with an exhortation to unite Christ's church in the truth rather than divide it. Smith's arguments are lucid and biblically powerful, and a sanctifying *treat* to the Christian's mind and soul. He quickly demonstrates the absurdity of that which is "not the true religion" of Jesus Christ and concretely sets down the *right religion* contained in Holy Scripture. So, reader, be inspired, as Smith *inspires us to a knowledge of the truth.*

In Christ and His immeasurable Grace
C. Matthew McMahon, April 2012
John 5:39, "...search the Scriptures..."
A Puritan's Mind
www.apuritanmind.com
www.puritanpublications.com
www.gracechapeltn.com

Meet Henry Smith
By C. Matthew McMahon, Ph.D., Th.D.

Henry Smith, who is apostrophized in Piers Penniless' Supplication (1592) as *Silver-tongued Smith*, was a celebrated preacher in Elizabethan London at St. Clement Danes. On leaving Queens' College, Cambridge, he continued his studies with Richard Greenham, rector of Dry Drayton, Cambridgeshire, who imbued him with Puritan principles as he did other leading men of the time. In 1575 he also entered Lincoln College, Oxford, graduating in 1579.

Though, as the eldest son and heir of Erasmus Smith of Somerby and Husbands Bosworth, Leicestershire, he was heir-apparent to a large patrimony, he prepared to enter the Ministry of the Church, but, owing to conscientious scruples on the matter of subscription, he determined not to undertake a pastoral charge, but to content himself with a Lectureship. Strype, in his Life of Bishop Aylmer, speaks of Smith as "an eloquent and witty man who in 1587 became Reader or Lecturer at St. Clement Danes, at the desire of many of the parishioners, and by the favor of the Lord Treasurer who dwelt in the same parish and yielded contribution to him."

Thomas Fuller also, in *A Life of Henry Smith* which he prefixed to the first *Collected Edition* of his works, said of him: "He was commonly called the Silver-tongued preacher, and that was but one metal below St. Chrysostom himself. His Church was so crowded with auditors that persons of good quality brought their own pews with them, I mean their legs, to stand thereon in the alleys. Their ears did so attend to his lips, their hearts to their ears, that he held the rudder of their affections in his hands, so that he could steer them whither he was pleased." Wood, too, tells us that Smith was "esteemed the miracle and wonder of his age, for his prodigious memory and for his fluent, eloquent and practical way of preaching." (*Athenae Oxon.* i. p. 603). And in our own time Marsden, in his *History of the Puritans*, has described Smith's Sermons as "noble examples of English prose and pulpit eloquence, and as being free in an astonishing degree from the besetting vices of his age—vulgarity and quaintness and affected learning."

Owing to ill-health he resigned his Lectureship about the end of 1590, and retired to Husbands Bosworth, where he died the following summer, and was buried July 4th, 1591, although some (like Brooks) place his death at

1600.

His *Collected Sermons* passed through the following editions:—1592, 1593, 1594, 1595, 1599, 1604, 1607, 1609, 1612, 1613, 1614, 1617, 1618, 1619, 1620, 1621, 1622, 1631 and 1632. Also added is Puritan Publications' first collection of his sermons in the work, "The Calling, Rebellion and Punishment of Jonah, and Other Sermons," which is a fantastic treatment of the book of Jonah. This current volume is specially designated to deal with lessons gleaned from the life of King Nebuchadnezzar, demonstrating how his pride opened the door to his fall, and then final restitution by God's grace. Smith's sermons in this work are outstanding, and though they are primarily relevant to kings, presidents and those in such authoritative position, they are equally relevant to Christians who must deal with the sins of pride and vainglory each day they live in this world regardless of their station in life.

J.B. and C.M.M.
March 1, 2013

CHAPTER 1: There is a God

That There is a God, and that He Ought to be Worshipped

Atheism and irreligion were ever odious even among the heathen themselves; insomuch as that Protagoras, for that he doubted whether there were any God or not, was by the Athenians banished out of their country. Diagoras was such a notorious infidel, that he held there was no God; him, and all such like Atheists, the very heathens have abhorred and detested, as being more like *rude beasts* than reasonable men. For Cicero, the heathen philosopher, condemns them all; and further says, *There was never any nation so savage, or people so barbarous, but always confessed that there was a God;*[2] to which they were led even by the light of nature, and natural instinct. For, the very same is confirmed by the common use of all heathens, in lifting up their eyes and hands to heaven, in any sudden distress that, comes upon them.[3] Yes, by experience of all ages, it has been proved that Atheists themselves, that is, such as in their health and prosperity, for more liberty of sinning, would strive against the being of a God when they came to die or fall into great misery, they of all others would show themselves most fearful of this God, as Seneca himself declares;[4] insomuch as Zeno the philosopher was accustomed to say, that it seemed to him a more

---

[2] Cicero, Lib. de Natura Deor.
[3] Tertul. In Apol.
[4] Seneca, De Ira, lib. i.

Chapter 1: That There is a God to Be Worshipped

substantial proof of this matter, to hear an Atheist at his dying day preach God, (when he asked God and all the world forgiveness,) than to hear all the philosophers in the world dispute the point: for that at this instant of death and misery, it is like that such speak in earnest and sobriety of spirit, who before in their wantonness impugned God.

It is remembered of Caius Caligula (that wicked and incestuous emperor) that he was a notable scorner and contemner of God, and made no reckoning of any other to be God but himself; yet this abominable and wicked Atheist, as God left him not unpunished; (for by His just judgment he was slain by some of his own officers): so while he lived, he was accustomed, (as the historiographers report of him,) at the terrible thundering and lightning, not only to cover his head, but also to get himself under his bed, and there to hide himself for fear.[5] Where (I pray you) this fear came upon him, but that his own conscience told him (howsoever in words perchance he would not affirm so much) that there was a God in heaven, able to quail and cast down his pride and all the emperors of the world, if He wishes, whose thunderbolts were so terrible as that justly by his own example he shown, He was to be feared of all the world? And of this it is that some say, that God is called *Deus*, of the Greek word, *Theos*, which signifies fear, because the fear of Him is planted and engrafted in the very natures and conscience

---

[5] Sueton. In Cal., 51; Dion in Caligula.

of all reasonable creatures, yes, even in the conscience of the greatest contemners and rankest Atheists of the world, who, say what they wish, and do what they wish, yet shall they never be able to root out this impression,—namely, *that there is a God*, whose fear is engraven in the hearts of *all men*.

And where (I pray you) comes shame in men after an offence committed? Or why should men (by natural instinct) put a difference between virtue and vice, good and evil, if there were not a God, who because He loved the one, and hated the other, has written that difference in every man's heart? Therefore conclude, that every man's knowledge, conscience, and feeling, is instead of a thousand witnesses to convince him (whosoever he is) that there is a God which is to be feared, which hates iniquity and wicked ways, and which in time of trouble and deep distress is to be sought to for refuge and relief, as the acts of the very *heathen* themselves do plainly demonstrate.

2. Moreover, as God is to be felt sensibly in every man's conscience, so is He to be seen visibly (if I may so speak) in the creation of the world, and of all things in it contained; for that this world had a beginning, all the excellent philosophers that ever were, have agreed, except Aristotle for a time, who held a fancy, that this world had no beginning, but was from all eternity; but at last, in his old age, he confessed and held the contrary, in his book *De Mundo*, which he wrote to King Alexander, (which book Justin Martyr esteemed greatly, and called it the epitome

Chapter 1: That There is a God to Be Worshipped

of all Aristotle's true philosophy).[6] This then being so, that the world had a beginning, it must necessarily follow, that it had an efficient Cause or Maker of it. I demand then, who it was that made it? If you say it made itself, it is absurd; for how could it make itself before itself was made, and when it had no being at all? If you say that something within the world made the world, that is, that some one part of the world made the whole, that is more absurd; for it is as much as if a man should say that the finger (and this before it was a finger or part of the body) did make the whole body. Wherefore it may be convinced by force of this argument (which is plainly demonstrative) that a greater and more excellent thing than is the whole world put together; yes, that something which was before heaven and earth were made, was and must necessarily be the Maker and Framer of this world; and this can be nothing else but GOD THE CREATOR OF ALL THINGS, who was before all His creatures, and is termed in the Sacred Writings, *Alpha and Omega*, "the first and the last," (Rev. 1:11); for that He only was without beginning Himself, and shall be and remain without ending: for He is eternal, being the *Primus Motor*, and the only Almighty Creator of all things. So true it is which Paul the Apostle testifies, when he says, "The invisible things of God, (that is, His eternal power and Divine essence,) are clearly seen, being understood by the things that are made," (Rom. 1:20). If therefore men would but cast up their eyes to heaven, and

---

[6] Vide Plutarch. De Placit Philos.; Aristot. De Mundo, lib. viii.; et vide Plot. De Mundo; Justin. In Apol.

from there look down again upon the earth, and so behold the excellent beauty and building of this world, they cannot be so sottish or dull conceited, but they must know there was and is a God which was the Maker of them, and be moved in some sort to glorify so incomparable and excellent a Creator. Yes, the poets and others have affirmed of God, that He is *Pater hominum*,—the Father of men, to show that men have their original and creation from Him; so that if we should draw our eyes from the beholding of the great world, and consider but man, (who for his beauty and excellency is called in Greek *Microcosmos*, the little world,) still we shall be enforced to acknowledge God the Author of us, the Father and Creator of us. So true is that which Paul the Apostle notes out of the poet Aratus, which says that *Ejus progenies sumus*, — We are the issue or "offspring" of God, (Acts 17:29). And as true it is, which he further says in that place, that "in Him we live, move, and have our being"; and therefore we owe all dutiful obedience and subjection unto Him, which duty and nature command us to perform in regard of our creation: for the son honours his father by natural duty, and all men are naturally carried to be grateful to their founders, to whom they are specially bound, and whom they ought not to forget, neither will they, except they be extremely unthankful and dissolute.

    3. Not only the creation of the world, and of all things in it contained, does proclaim that there is a God, who is to be honoured for His infinite extended authority and almighty power, (for He made all things of nothing,

only He spoke the word, and they were created,) but His daily blessings and benefits sent down upon the earth, do show also there is a God, which is provident, and has care of men, and therefore of men to be praised, thanked, and glorified forever: for true it is which St. Paul says in this behalf, that "God left not Himself without witness, in that He did good, and gave us rain from heaven, and fruitful seasons, filling our hearts with food and gladness," (Acts 14:17). By means of these and all other His blessings, men might, and still may daily be induced not only to believe that there is a God from whom they receive all these, but also to acknowledge and attribute all praise and thanksgiving unto Him, as to their first principal and special Benefactor; for the *ox doth know his owner, and the ass his master's crib*, (Isa. 1:3). And therefore how can it be but reasonable men should much more know God, not only their first Founder and Creator, but their daily Feeder, Preserver, Keeper, and Upholder? for so often as they think upon these things, and see and have them, they cannot choose but be put in mind of God—the Sender and Author of them all, and be moved with a grateful mind towards Him. And hereof it is that He is called *Deus a dando*,—of giving; and in English we call God, *quasi Good*, because He is only and perfectly good of Himself alone, and the Giver of all goodness, and of all good gifts and blessings unto others; from whom, as from the fountain, all benefits whatsoever do come, descend, flow, and be derived to them, (Matt. 19:17; James 1:17; Rom. 9:16).

4. I might here show how God is also known to the

world by His judgments upon wicked and unrighteous people, whom divers times He makes visible examples of His severity and justice (if men did well consider them); for hereby also has God manifested Himself, as Paul the Apostle teaches. These premises, I trust, may *suffice*, (if there were no more to be said); for by them we may easily see and prove that there is a God which created the world, and all things in it; which preserves and upholds the same with His mighty puissance, supports the earth, and all the creatures of it, with His providence and helping hand: yes, besides the heavens and the earth, which are the work of His hands, every man's own conscience plentifully teaches (as I said before) that there is a God which is to be *feared*: for howsoever many a man that has spent his life in a wicked way, and most damnable course, could wish in his heart there were no God, because he sees God no otherwise than in His vengeance; yes, howsoever many a wicked person soothes himself in his wickedness, and flatteringly says to himself, (like the fool in the Psalms,) "There is no God," (Psa. 14:1); yet at other times his own conscience will so provoke him, and enforce this matter, (that there is a God,) that with horror and dread of Him, it will make him quake, fear, and tremble; for the fear of Him is so deeply printed in the natures of all men, as that it is impossible to shake it off; and which is more, a kind of devotion to worship Him, being the Creator and Preserver of men, and of all things else, and the provident Father of all, is planted and inseparably fixed in the hearts of all men, though all men of all nations does not know how to

Chapter 1: That There is a God to Be Worshipped

worship Him aright, and in such sort as He requires. This is manifest by the examples of all nations and people in the world, who all have some one kind of religion or other, though all do not find the *right* religion. All be devoted to the worship of God, howsoever all do not find out the true God, nor His right manner of worship, but worship Him according to the devices of their own brain.

Considering then that there is no nation under the sun so barbarous (nor ever was) but aimed at the worship of God, and either worshipped Him, or something else in His place, it appears to be a most vain and foolish conceit which Atheists sometimes utter, namely, that religion is nothing else but a matter of policy, or a politic device of human invention; for it is evident, that religious affection to worship God is naturally seated (and ever was) in the hearts of all men; and the conscience of every man, even of the greatest scorner and contemner of God, which sometimes trembles before His judgment-seat, abundantly testifies, that a religious devotion of fear towards God is bred and born with every man; and therefore it cannot be any policy of human invention, inasmuch as if there were no laws of men, yet this religious affection to worship God, and the fear of Him, would and does remain written by the finger of God in the hearts and consciences of all men living, how rude, savage, or barbarous soever they are. What law of men (I pray) was there, to make Caligula the emperor, when he heard the terrible thundering in the air, and saw the flashing flames of lightning about him, to run under his bed, and to hide himself for fear of this terrible and great God? or what makes the rankest Atheist in the world in the like case, and at the like tempest, to do the like? or what made the heathens in any dangerous or sudden distress to lift up their eyes or hands to heaven, mightily to fear and to be astonished? None can say it is the law of men, for no law of men enforces this attempt; but it is a natural instinct of the fear of God, (whom he has offended, and whose vengeance he dreadeth, and from whom he thinks succor may come,) seated in all men's hearts even from their nativity, which makes him to fear, and cause him to seek to God for refuge. Let this, therefore, remain firm and most undoubted,— THAT THE FEAR OF THE GREAT GOD, AND A RELIGIOUS DISPOSITION TO WORSHIP THE SAME GOD, IS NOT ENFORCED BY THE LAWS OF MEN, BUT NATURALLY SOWN IN THE HEARTS OF ALL MEN, THOUGH ALL DO NOT FIND OUT, NOR OBSERVE THE RIGHT RELIGION.

Let us, therefore, now seek and search out which is the *true religion*, which is acceptable to God, and which is without wavering and doubting, and is to be observed of men: for all nations and people have a kind of religion, (as I said before,) but all do not have the true and right religion.

CHAPTER 2: Christianity the Only True Religion

In which, and in the Next Chapter, is Shown that the Christian Religion is the Only True Religion in the World, and Wherewith Only God is Pleased

In ancient times all the world was divided and distinguished into Jews and Gentiles; and this distinction does, and may still, remain among us; if therefore I can prove the truth of this our Christian religion against both Jews and Gentiles, I shall then prove it against all the world. In this chapter I will first prove it against the Jews, and in the next against the Gentiles. Concerning the Jews, they will easily grant our religion to be the true religion, if we can prove Jesus Christ (whom we believe to be that Messiah) was foretold by their prophets, being the true and undoubted prophets of God. And this we are sure may easily be proved; and therefore in vain do the Jews look for any other Messiah than He that is already come, namely, Jesus Christ our Mediator, Saviour, and Redeemer, in whom God, His Father, is well-pleased, and for whose sake (if we believe in Him) He will not be offended with us, but be reconciled to us and save us. Whatsoever was foretold to belong to their Messiah, is fully performed and perfectly accomplished in our Jesus Christ, and in no other; and therefore our Jesus was and is the true Messiah, and no other. Let us in this consider the marks of the Messiah, by which He might be known; and so shall we see that our

Saviour Jesus Christ is the only true Messiah, and none but He.

1. One mark for us to know the Messiah by, is, that when He came, He should not be known or acknowledged to be the Messiah, but should be *rejected* and *refused* of the Jewish nation, to the end He might be put to death amongst them, according to the, "fore-appointment and determinate counsel of God," (Acts 2:23), for had they received Him for the Messiah, they would never have used Him so shamefully as they did, neither should He then have been slain amongst them, as was foretold He should. This then being one mark of the Messiah,—that He should be refused for the Messiah of the Jewish nation, and of the chiefest rulers amongst them, is a great confirmation of our faith, inasmuch as it is found fully performed in our Saviour Jesus Christ, whom they scorned, rejected, condemned, and put to death. And therefore, if the Jewish nation had received bur Jesus for the Messiah, it had been an undoubted argument that He had not been the right Messiah; so on the other side, because they did refuse Him, it is a very strong persuasion to us that He was, and is, the very true Messiah indeed. In vain, therefore, it is, if any do look for such a Messiah as should be wholly received of the Jewish nation; for none such was promised, yes, it was foretold (contrariwise) that He should be refused of them, as our Jesus was; that so He might be made an offering for sin, according to the preordination of God.

2. It was foretold of the Messiah, that He should be born of a Virgin, (Isa. 7:14); that the place of His birth

Chapter 2: That The Christian Religion is The True Religion

should be Bethlehem, (Mic. 5:2); that at His birth all the infants round about Bethlehem should be slain for His sake, (Jer. 31:15) that the kings of the earth should come and adore Him, and offer gold and other gifts to Him, (Psa. 72:10); that He should be presented in the temple of Jerusalem, for the greater glory of the second temple, (Mal. 3:1); that He should fly into Egypt, and be recalled thence again, (Hos. 11:1); that a star should appear at His birth, to notify His coming into the world, (Num. 24:17); that John the Baptist (who came in the spirit and power of Elias, and therefore was called Elias, Luke 1:17; Matt. 11:10, 34) should be the messenger to go before Him, and to prepare the way, and to cry in the desert, (Mal. 3:1; Mark 1:2); after this, that He should begin His own preaching with all humility, quietness, and clemency of spirit, (Isa. 13:2); that He should be poor, abject, and of no reputation in this world, (Isa. 53; Dan. 9:26; Zech. 9:9) that He should do strange miracles, and heal all diseases, (Isa. 59:1); that He should die and be slain for the sins of His people, (Dan. 9:26; Isa. 53); that He should be betrayed by one that put his hand in the dish with Him, and was His own disciple, (Psa. 12:9; 55:13, 14); that He should be sold for thirty pieces of silver, (Zech. 11:12); that with those thirty pieces, there should be bought afterwards a field of potsherds, (Zech. 11:13); that He should ride into Jerusalem upon an ass before His passion, (Zech. 9:9); that the Jews should beat, and buffet His face, and defile the same with spitting upon it, (Isa. 50:6); that they should whip His body before they put Him to death, (Isa. 53:4); that they should put Him to death among thieves and malefactors, (Isa. 53:12); that they should give Him vinegar to drink, divide His apparel, and cast lots for His upper garment, (Psa. 22:18); that the manner of His death should be crucifixion, that is, nailing of His hands and His feet upon the cross, (Psa. 22:16); that His side should be pierced, and that they should look upon Him when they had so pierced Him, (Zech. 12:10); that He should rise again from death the third day, (Psa. 16:10); that He should ascend into heaven, and sit at the right hand of His Father, in glory and royalty, and like a conquering potentate over-ruling all, (Psa. 110:1-2). *All these things and whatsoever else belonging to the Messiah, are found perfectly fulfilled in Jesus Christ, and in no other.* And therefore He alone, and no other, is the true Messiah.

3. To this have I spoken of such circumstances and accidents, as did belong to the Messiah, concerning His incarnation, birth, life, death, burial, resurrection, and ascension into heaven, and there sitting at the right hand of His Father; and also of His rejection by Jews, and the Jewish nation; which things albeit they be very wonderful, and sufficient to establish any man's belief in Christ Jesus our Lord, in whom only they are found faithfully fulfilled; yet if we shall consider with this THE TIME OF THE MESSIAH'S APPEARING, and when He should come into the world, our faith will be so much the more confirmed towards Him.

Daniel the prophet of God (who lived in the time of the first monarchy) foretold that there should be three monarchies more, and the last of these four monarchies greatest of all; and that in the days of this fourth and last monarchy (which was the Roman monarchy or empire) the Eternal King, or Messiah, should come, and build up God's kingdom throughout all the world. (Dan. 2:39, 44). And this happened accordingly; for Jesus came, and was born in the fourth monarchy, (which was the Roman,) namely, in the days of Augustus the Roman emperor. But yet let us go more strictly to the matter.

  The temple of Jerusalem (as all men know) was built twice; first by King Solomon, which lasted about four hundred and forty years, and then was destroyed by Nebuchadnezzar King of Babylon; wherefore about seventy years after, it was builded again by Zerubbabel, who reduced the Jews from their captivity. But this second temple, for pomp and riches of the material building, was nothing like to the first, (which the old men in the Book of Ezra do testify by their weeping), when they saw this second, and remembered the first, (Ezra 3:12, 13,) and which Haggai the Prophet expressly testifies, (Hag. 2:3). And yet says God by His Prophet Haggai in the same place, "that after a while the Desire of all nations shall come; and I will fill this house with glory, saith the Lord of hosts. The glory of this latter house shall be greater than of the former," (Hag. 2:7, 9): which prophecy was fulfilled by the coming of our Saviour Jesus Christ into this second temple; which being personally done, was of far greater dignity, and more glory to it, than any dignity whatsoever was found in the first temple builded by Solomon. It is therefore manifest that the Desire of all nations, that is, the

Messiah, should come whilst the second temple stood. And so Daniel also shows, that the second temple (after the building of it) should not be destroyed until the Messiah were first come and slain, (Dan. 9:26). And Malachi the Prophet also most plainly testifies, that He should come during the second temple, (Mal. 3:1). And so indeed He did: for Christ Jesus came into the world during that second temple, and did Himself likewise foretell the destruction of it, ere that generation passed, which came to pass accordingly; for it was destroyed about forty-six years after the ascension of our Saviour into heaven, by Titus, son to Vespasian, the Roman emperor. Most vainly therefore do the Jews, or any other, expect for a Messiah to come, *after the destruction of that second temple.*

Let us yet moreover consider the prophecy of old Jacob concerning the particular time of the Messiah's appearing: "And Jacob called unto his sons, and said, Gather yourselves together that I may tell you that which shall befall you in the last days. The sceptre shall not depart from Judah, nor a lawgiver from between his feet, until Shiloh come; and unto Him shall the gathering of the people be," (Gen. 49:1, 10). By *Shiloh* is meant the Messiah (as both Jews and Christians expound it). This prophecy, so long foretold, was performed at the birth of Jesus Christ, in the days of Herod King of Jewry: for from the time that the sceptre was given to King David, (who was the first king of the tribe of Judah,) it did not depart from that tribe, but remained always in it, until the days of King Herod in whose time, and not until whose time, all government was

Chapter 2: That The Christian Religion is The True Religion

taken away and clean departed from the tribe of Judah, and committed to a stranger; and therefore in the time of Herod was the Messiah to be born, and neither before nor after his time. That the sceptre, or government, was not clean taken away or departed from the house of Judah, (after it was once settled in it, in the person of King David,) even till the days of Herod the King, is evident; for from David (who was the first king of that tribe) to Zedekiah that died in the captivity of Babylon, the Scripture shows how all the kings descended of the house of Judah. And during the time of their captivity in Babylon (which was seventy years) the Jews were always permitted to choose to themselves a governor of the house of Judah (whom they called *Reschgalut*).[7] And after their delivery from Babylon, Zerubbabel was their governor of the same tribe; and so others after him until you come to the Maccabees, who were both governors and priests, (1 Esd. 1:23; 1 Mac. 2, 3,) for that they were of the mother's side of the tribe of Judah, and by the father's side of the tribe of Levi, (as Rabbi Kimchi observeth,)[8] and so from these men down to Hireanus King of Jewry, who was the last king which was lineally descended of the house of David, and of the tribe of Judah. For after Hireanus, came the aforenamed Herod, a mere stranger, whose father (as Josephus, who well knew, reporteth)[9] was called Antipater, and came out of Idumea: he came into acquaintance and favour with the Romans,

---

[7] Sambed., cap. Dinei Manmouth; Rab. Moses Aegypt., in Praefat.; Maimon.
[8] Rab. Kimchi, Com. In Agg.
[9] Joseph. Antiq., lib. i. 1, 3, 14.

partly by his said father's means; (who was, as Josephus says, a well-moneyed man, industrious, and factious); and partly by his own diligence and ambition, being of himself both witty, beautiful, and of most excellent and rare qualities, by which commendations he came at length to marry the daughter of Hireanus aforesaid, King of Jewry, and by this marriage obtained of his father-in-law to be chief governor and ruler of the province and land of Galilee under him. But Hireanus afterward, in a battle against the Parthians, fell into their hands, and was taken and carried prisoner into Parthia. Herod then took his journey to Rome, and there he obtained to be created King of Jewry, without any title or interest in the world; for that not only his father-in-law, Hireanus, was then living in Parthia, but that also his younger brother Aristobulus, and three of his sons, (viz., Antigonus, Alexander, Aristobulus,) with divers others of the blood royal in Jewry, were alive also.[10] Herod then having procured by this means to be King of Jewry, procured first to have in his hands the King Hireanus, and so put him to death. He brought also to the same end his younger brother Aristobulus, and his three sons likewise. He put to death also his own wife Mariamnes, which was King Hireanusl s daughter, as also Alexandra her mother, and soon after two of his own sons, which he had by the same Mariamnes, for that they were of the blood royal of Judah; and a little after that again, he put to death his third son, named Antipater. He caused also to be slain forty of the chiefest noblemen of the same

---

[10] Joseph. Antiq., lib. xv.

Chapter 2: That The Christian Religion is The True Religion

tribe of Judah. And as Philo the Jew (who lived at the same time with him) writes, *He put to death all the Sanhedrin*; that is, the twenty-seven senators, or elders, of the tribe of Judah that rules the people. He killed the chief of the sect of the Pharisees. He burned the genealogies of all the kings and princes of the house of Judah, and caused one Nicolaus Damascenus, an historiographer, that was his servant, to draw out a pedigree for him and his line, as though he had descended from the ancient kings of Judah. He translated the priesthood, and sold it to strangers. And finally, he so razed, dispersed, and mangled the house of Judah, in such sort, as no one jot of government or principality remained in it. Now then in the days of this King Herod, and not till then, was the sceptre, that is, the government, departed from Judah: and therefore then, and not till then, was the Messiah to appear, according to that prophecy of Jacob; and so it came to pass accordingly: for Christ Jesus the true and undoubted Messiah was then born, viz., in the time of Herod King of Jewry. In vain therefore do the Jews, or any other, look for any other Messiah to come after the days of that Herod, in whose time (and not before) was the sceptre and all principality and government departed utterly from the house of Judah; and therefore in his time, and neither before nor after, was the Messiah to appear and come, according to Jacob's prophecy.

  Daniel the Prophet yet goes nearer to work, and foreshows even the very day, and time of the day, when the Messiah should be slain for the sins of the people; for in the first year of Darius, son of Ahasuerus, King of the Medes, about the time of the evening oblation, he prayed to God for the people and their deliverance, inasmuch as then he perceived that the seventy years of their captivity (foretold by Jeremiah) were now come to an end. So Daniel thus praying, about that time of the evening oblation, God sent His angel Gabriel to signify and show to him, that at the very beginning of his supplications the commandment came forth for the return of the people from their captivity, and to build again Jerusalem; and shows likewise, that as the people had now been in the captivity of Babylon seventy years, and then were delivered from that their earthly bondage; so it should come to pass, that within seventy weeks of years the Messiah should come, who should finish wickedness, seal up sins, blot out iniquity, and bring in everlasting righteousness, and be a deliverer not only from the outward, but from the spiritual Babylon, and hellish Egypt. The words of the angel are these following:

> "At the beginning of thy supplications the commandment came forth, and I am come to shew thee; for thou art greatly beloved: therefore understand the matter, and consider the vision. Seventy weeks are determined upon thy people, and upon thy holy city, to finish the transgression, and to make an end of sins, and to make reconciliation for iniquity, and to bring in everlasting righteousness, and to seal up the vision and prophecy, and to anoint the Most Holy. Know

therefore and understand, that from the going forth of the commandment to restore and to build Jerusalem unto Messiah the Prince, shall be seven weeks, and threescore and two weeks, *etc.* After threescore and two weeks shall Messiah be cut off, but not for Himself, *etc.* He shall confirm the covenant with many for one week; and in the midst of the week He shall cause the sacrifice and the oblation to cease," (Dan. 9:23–27).

For the better understanding of which words, it must be remembered that this word *Hebdomada*, signifying a week or seven, is sometimes taken for a week of days, that is, seven days; and then it is called *Hebdomada dierum*,—a week of days; as in this prophecy of Daniel he says of himself that he did mourn three weeks of days, (Dan. 10:2): but at other times it signifies the space of seven years, and that is called *Hebdomada annorum*,—a week of years, as in Lev. 25:8, where it is said, "Thou shalt number seven sabbaths of years unto thee, seven times seven years; and the space shall be unto thee forty and nine years." Now it is most certain that these seventy weeks are to be understood of weeks of years, and not of days, for that even by the Jews' own confession, as also by the Book of Ezra, it is manifest, that the temple and Jerusalem were many years in building before they were finished. These seventy weeks of years therefore are seven times seventy years, which makes in a sum total,—four hundred and ninety years, within which time the Messiah should be slain; for from the going forth of the commandment to bring the people back again, and to build Jerusalem, (which commandment went forth at the beginning of his supplications, which were the first year of Darius, as the text shows,) to the time that Messiah the Prince was anointed to preach the kingdom of God, (which was after His baptism, when He began to be about thirty years of age,) there must be seven weeks, and threescore and two weeks, that is forty and nine weeks, which make four hundred fourscore and three years; which number of years being rightly accounted from that time of Darius, in which the commandment went forth, are fully accomplished in the fifteenth year of Tiberius Caesar, at which time Christ Jesus was baptized and anointed by the Spirit of God, descending down upon Him in the form of a dove, a voice also being heard from heaven, saying, "This is My beloved Son in whom I am well pleased," (Matt. 3:17). Yet is there one week more to make up the number of seventy, in the midst of which week the Messiah should be slain, which came to pass accordingly; for in the midst of that week, that is, about three years and a half after Christ's baptism, Christ Jesus the true Messiah was put to death, and died for our sins, which was in the eighteenth year of Tiberius Caesar. In vain, therefore do the Jews or any other look for another Messiah to come, after the days of that Tiberius Caesar, the Roman emperor.

4. The Scriptures do show that the Messiah should come *of the seed of David*, according to the words of God, "I have sworn by My holiness that I will not lie unto David. His seed shall endure for ever, and His throne as the sun

before Me," (Psa. 89:35, 36), which cannot be applied to King Solomon his son (as the latter Jews apply it); for these words cannot be verified in Solomon, whose earthly kingdom was rent and torn in pieces straight after his death by Jeroboam, and not long after as it were extinguished; neither can they be understood of any terrestrial king; but they must necessarily be understood of an Eternal King, which should come of David's seed. The promise then made to David for Christ to come of his seed is again repeated after his death by many Prophets, and confirmed by God; as in Jeremiah, where God uses these words, "Behold, the days come that I will raise unto David a righteous Branch, and a King shall reign and prosper, and shall execute judgment and justice in the earth. In His days shall Judah be saved, and Israel shall dwell safely: and this is His name by which He shall be called, THE LORD OUR RIGHTEOUSNESS," (Jer. 23:5, 6; 33:16). All this was spoken of David above four hundred years after David was dead; which proves manifestly that the promises and speeches were not made to King David, for Solomon his son, nor for any other temporal king of David's line, but for Christ, who was particularly called the Son of David; for that David was the first king of the tribe of Judah, and not only was Christ's progenitor in the flesh, but also did bear His type and figure in many other things. For which cause likewise in Ezekiel (who lived about the same time that Jeremiah did) the Messiah is called by the name of David himself; for thus says God at that time to Ezekiel, "I will save My flocks and they shall no more be a prey; I will set over them a shepherd, and He shall feed them, even My servant David; He shall feed them, and He shall be their shepherd, and I the Lord will be their God, and My servant David shall be a Prince among them," (Ezek. 34:22–24). In which words, not only we that are Christians, but the latter Jews also themselves do confess in the Talmud, that their Messiah is called David, for that He was to descend of his seed. Now then let us see whether Jesus Christ our Lord did come of the seed of David, as was foretold the Messiah should. It is plain that He did, for never any man doubted or denied but that Jesus was directly of the tribe of Judah, and descended lineally, by His mother, of the only house of David (as was foretold He should); which is confirmed most clearly by the two genealogies and pedigrees set down by St. Matthew and St. Luke, of the blessed virgin, whose descent was from David, and Joseph was of the same tribe and kindred with her; (Matt. 1; Luke 3); for according to the law of the Jews, they used to marry in their own tribe. And therefore the Evangelists, showing the line of Joseph, do thereby also declare the lineage and stock of Mary, (the mother of Jesus,) as being a thing then sufficiently known to all, though they spoke no more. It is also confirmed by their repairing to Bethlehem, (when commandment was given by Augustus Caesar, that every one should repair to the head-city of their tribe and family, to be taxed or assessed for their tribute, Luke 2:1, 5) for by their going thither it is shown, that they were both of the lineage of David, inasmuch as Bethlehem was the proper city only of them that were of the house and lineage of

David, for that King David was born in it. Moreover, it may appear by this, for that the Jews who sought out all exception they could against Him, yet never excepted this, nor alleged against Him, that He was not of the house of Judah, nor of the house of David; which they would never have omitted, if they might have done it with any color; for such a speech (if it could truly have been spoken) would easily have convinced our Jesus not to be the true Messiah. But it appears they never doubted this. Yes, I add further, that it remains registered in the Jews' Talmud itself, that Jesus of Nazareth, crucified, was of the blood royal, from Zerubbabel of the house of David.[11] Wherewith agree that saying of Paul the Apostle, where he testifies thus, "Jesus Christ our Lord was made of the seed of David according to the flesh; and declared to be the Son of God with pouter, according to the Spirit of holiness," (Rom. 1:3, 4).

5. That the mother of Jesus was a virgin, is plentifully testified by the Evangelists; and that so the Messiah's mother should be, the Scriptures of the Jews do sufficiently show: for in Isa. 7:14, it is told as a strange thing to King Ahaz (and so it is indeed) that a virgin should conceive and bring forth a Son, and they should call his name Emmanuel, that is, God with us: (Matt. 1:23): which could not be strange, if the Hebrew word in that place did signify only a young woman; (as some later *rabbins* do affirm); for that is no strange or new thing, but common and ordinary, for young women to conceive and bear children. Wherefore the Septuagint do rightly translate

---

[11] Tal. Tract. Sab. Cap. Higmar.

the word *parthenos*, which properly and fully signifies *a virgin*, and so did also the elder Jews understand it, as Rabbi Simeon well notes.[12] And Rabbi Moses Hadarsan, (of singular credit among the Jews,) upon these words of the Psalm, "Truth shall spring out of the earth," says, that it is not said, *Truth shall be engendered of the earth*, but *Truth shall spring forth*, to signify thereby that the Messiah (who is meant by the word *Truth*) shall not be begotten as other men in carnal copulation;[13] he also cites Rabbi Berechius to be of the same opinion; and finally Rabbi Hacadosch proves by art cabalistical out of many places of Scripture, not only that the mother of the Messiah shall be a virgin, but also that her name shall be Mary.[14] Like as also the same Rabbi Hacadosch proves by the same art out of many texts of Scripture, that the Messiah's name at His coming shall be Jesus.[15] And that the mother of the Messiah should be a virgin, may further appear in the Prophecy of Jeremiah, where God says, "I will create a new thing in the earth, a woman shall compass a man," (Jer. 31:22); which were no new thing, but usual and accustomed, except he understood of a *virgin* that should bear a child.

6. Now because Christ Jesus by the wonderful works and surpassing miracles which He did, being such as no man could do, (if He had been but a bare man,) as also by His heavenly doctrine, words, and deeds, did

---

[12] Rab. Sim. Ben. Johai, in Gen. 2:20.
[13] Rab. Moses Hadars., in Psa. 85.
[14] Rab. Hacad., ad qu. 3, in Isa. 9.
[15] Rab. Hacad., in Isa. 9.

declare Himself to be the Son of God, sent from the bosom of His Father, let us also, as we have found the Messiah to be man, so search whether he ought not to be God also. The sacred Scriptures of the Jews give answer, that he ought to be God also, and so to be both God and man: which thing is signified by the Prophet Isaiah, when he says, "They shall call His name Immanuel," (Isa. 7:14) "which is by interpretation, God with us," (Matt. 1:23). Again, the same Isaiah testifies, "that they shall call His name, Wonderful, Counsellor, the mighty God, the everlasting Father, the Prince of Peace," (Isa. 9:6). Again by Isaiah He is called, the issue of the Lord, and also the fruit of the earth, to signify Him to be both the Son of God, and the Son of man. (Isa. 4:2). And Jeremiah the Prophet testifies of Him, that "He shall be called the Lord our righteousness," (Jer. 23:6; 32:26). And God Himself says of Him, "Thou art My Son; this day have I begotten Thee," (Psa. 2:7). And David proves Him plainly to be the Son of God; for though he knew He should come of his seed as touching the flesh, yet he also calls Him his Lord, saying in this way, "The Lord said unto my Lord, Sit thou at My right hand till I make Thine enemies Thy footstool," (Psa. 110:1). Since David calls Him his Lord, it is manifest that he makes Him not only to be man, but God also, even the Son of God, the second Person in the Trinity. This matter is testified almost everywhere in the Scripture of the Jews, and therefore I need no further to amplify.

7. Yet because the Jews do look for the Messiah to be a terrestrial King which should reign in Jewry, and

subdue all the enemies with His terrestrial power and force, in which how grossly they err, as the premises do partly show, so is it not impertinent here to speak somewhat to convince their so gross an opinion. For first, the time is past long ago in which the Messiah should come, and yet no such terrestrial king as they dream of has been reigning in Jewry; and therefore very experience and knowledge of the times might teach them to abandon so foolish a conceit. Daniel calls Him "the eternal King," (Dan. 2:44). Micah says, "He shall reign even for ever," (Mic. 4:7); which cannot be supposed of an earthly kingdom. Again, "Ask of Me, (*God says to His Son the Messiah,*) and I will give Thee the heathen for Thine inheritance, and the uttermost part of the earth for Thy possession," (Psa. 2:8); which words do show, that the Messiah should be a universal King, to rule not only over the Jews, but over the Gentiles also, even over all the world. Again it is said, "His name shall endure for ever. He shall have dominion from sea to sea, unto the ends of the earth. All kings shall fall down before Him; all nations shall serve Him," (Psa. 72). And it was told Abraham, that in his seed (that is, in the Messiah which should come of his seed) "all nations of the earth should be blessed," (Gen. 18:18); how then should He overthrow any nation for the Jews' sake (as they dream) when all nations were to receive their blessing from Him? In the Prophecy of Isaiah, the commission of God His Father to Him is thus set down: It is a light thing that Thou shouldest be My servant to raise up the tribes of Jacob, and to restore the preserved of Israel; "I will also give Thee for a light to the Gentiles, that Thou mayest be My salvation unto the end of the earth," (Isa. 49:6). Everywhere almost it is testified, that the Gentiles should have every way as much interest in the Messiah as the Jews, and He should be as beneficial to them. The Messiah, therefore, though He be termed a King, and is so indeed, yet is to be supposed a spiritual and eternal King, (as the Prophets declare Him,) for it is too childish and fond to imagine Him to be an earthly King, which should reign only in Judea, and be a great and mighty and terrestrial Conqueror. Does not Zechariah (as touching His estate in this world) show that He should come poorly, riding upon an ass? (Zech. 9:9). Does not Isaiah say, that in this world He should be a man despised, abject, and of no reputation? (Isa. 53:3). Does not Daniel expressly say that He should come to be slain, that with His sacrifice He might take away sin, and cease all other sacrifices? (Dan. 9:26, 27). Does not Zechariah say, that they should look upon Him after they had pierced or crucified Him? (Zech. 12:10). And does not the Prophet Isaiah say of Him, that He gave His soul an offering for sin, and that He should be led as a sheep to the slaughter, and as a lamb dumb before his shearer, so opened He not His mouth? (Isa. 53). Where then is His pomp, when He was to be poor? Where was His earthly honour, when He was to be abject and of no reputation? Where was His worldly conquest, when He was Himself to be slain? Where should His fleshly resistance be, when He was not so much as to offer it, yes, when His enemies were to lead Him to death as the sheep to the slaughter, and as a lamb dumb before his shearer, not opening His mouth to save Himself? Yes, how should the Jews think (if they would thoroughly consider) that the Messiah should be such a one as they dream of, when they were the men that should pursue Him to death, and whom they should look upon when they had pierced Him?

These things which have been spoken (though in very brief and plain sort) are, I trust, sufficient to convince the Jews that our Lord and Saviour Jesus Christ is that Seed of the woman which should break the serpent's head, which deceived Adam and Eve our first parents; and He in whom all the nations of the earth should be blessed, and is in all points the very true, certain, and undoubted Messiah, which was fore-promised and foretold by their Prophets; for all things which were foretold of the Messiah, do fitly, fully, and only agree to Him, and to no other. And therefore I conclude against them, that the Christian religion which we profess, and which we hold derived to us from that Christ the true Messiah (the Author of it) is the only true religion which is acceptable to God.

CHAPTER 3: Against Infidels

In which is Shown that the Christian Religion is the Only True Religion, Against the Gentiles, and all Infidels of the World

That there is a God, the heathen have evermore confessed, that there is but one God (as the Christian religion holdeth) all the learned sort of the heathen philosophers have acknowledged; for howsoever they dissembled at some times, and applied themselves outwardly to the error of the vulgar sort, in naming of gods, yet surely they never spoke of more than of one God. Which thing may appear by Plato in an Epistle which he writes to Dionysius King of Sicily, in which he gives him a sign when he spoke in jest, and when in earnest; *Hinc disces tu scribam ego serio necne; cum serio, ordior epistolam ab uno Deo; cam secus, a pluribus.* By this (he says) you shall know whether I write in earnest or not; for when I write in earnest, I begin my letter with one God; and when I write not in earnest, I do begin my letter in the name of many Gods.[16] And three of the most learned that ever professed the Platonic sect, Plotinus, Porphyrius, and Preclus, do all testify and prove in divers parts of their works (being themselves but heathens) that both themselves, and their master Plato, never believed indeed but one God.[17]

---

[16] Plato, Epist. 13, ad Dionys.
[17] Plotin. Enneae i. lib. viii., 1, 2; et En. vi. lib. iv., cap. 12, 3, 4. Porph. De Abst., lib. ii.; et De Occa., cap. 2. Procl. in Theolog. Platon.; et Lib. de Anima et Daem., i., 31, 42, 55.

Aristotle that ensued Plato, and began the Sect of the *Peripatetics*, though he were a man so much given to the search of nature, as that sometime he seemed to forget God, the Author of Nature; yet in his old age, when he wrote the Book of the World, he resolves the matter more clearly, acknowledging also one God; and says moreover in the same place, that the multitude of gods was invented to express the power of this one God, by the multitude of His ministers.[18] By which appears, that like the more foolish sort of heathens did imagine of God as of earthly princes; for they saw that every earthly prince had a great many men ministers, otherwise called servants, and attendants upon him, by this to declare and shows his power, his magnificence, and high honour; and therefore they thought likewise, that the great and high God could not be sufficiently conceived of, except it were supposed that He had a great number of inferior gods, waiting and attending upon Him, in like sort to show His greatness and magnificence. This opinion of their master concerning one God, Theophrastus and Aphrodiseus, two principal Peripatetics, do confirm at large.[19]

Zeno, the chief and father of all the Stoics, was accustomed to say, (as Aristotle himself reporteth,) that either one God, or no God. Which opinion of one God is averred everywhere by Plutarch and Seneca, two most excellent writers, and great admirers of the Stoic severity. And before them by Epictetus, a man of singular account

---

[18] Arist. De Mundo.
[19] Theoph. In Metaph.; Alex. Aphrod. De Provid.

Chapter 3: Against the Gentiles and All Infidels

in that sect, whose words were esteemed oracles: *Dicendum ante omnia, unum esse Deum, omnia regere, omnibus providere.* Before all things (he says) we must affirm that there is one God, and that this God governs all, and has providence over all.

As for the Academics, although their usage was to doubt and dispute every thing, as Cicero seems to do in his discourse concerning the gods; yet at last he concludes in this point with the Stoics, who believed one God.[20] And as for Socrates, who was the father and founder of the Academic sect, (and who was judged by the oracle of Apollo to be the wisest man in all Greece) the world knows that he was put to death for jesting at the multitude of gods among the Gentiles.[21]

All these four sects of philosophers then (who in their time bare the credit of learning) made (as we see) profession of one God, when they came to speak as they thought. And yet if we will ascend up higher to the days before these sects began, that is, to Pythagoras, and Archytas Tarentinus, and before them again to Mercurius Trismegistus, that was the first parent of philosophy to the Egyptians, we shall find them so plain and resolute in this, as none can be more. It is true that the heathen did honour such men as were famous (either for their valiant acts, their singular invention in matters, their good turns to others, or their own rare gifts and qualities above others) with the title of gods; but yet they believed not that those

---

[20] Cicero De Natura Deor.
[21] Apuleius, Alleg.; et Laert. in Vita Socrat.

men were gods; yes, they knew them to be no other than mortal men, which thing Trismegistus shows, when he says, *Dem non naturce ratione, sed honoris causa nominamus;—* We name them gods not in respect of their natures, but for honour's sake.[22] That is, we call them gods, not for that we think them to be so, but because under that title we would honour some famous acts, or rare parts and qualities which were in them. Cicero likewise testifies the same in these words: The life of man (he says) and common custom, have now received to lift up to heavenly fame and good-will such men as for their good turns are accounted excellent; and hereof it comes, that Hercules, Castor and Pollux, Aesculapius, and Liber, (which were but men,) are now reckoned for gods.[23] Perseus likewise, Zeno's scholar, testifies the same: and therefore did the Grecians truly think, who (as Herodotus reporteth)[24] thought that their gods (whom they so called) were no other at first than mortal men, and so is the common opinion of all. And when men and women that were famous, excellent, and surpassing others, died, because the memory of them should not die with them, but remain as precedents to follow, or as persons to be admired at; those that were living could not be content to honour them with the title of gods and goddesses, but also would needs have their pictures or images drawn, and set up somewhere for posterity to behold. Hereof it came, that they after a while

---

[22] Triam. in Paeman., cap; 2-5, &c.; in Asclep:, c. 26, &c.
[23] Cicero's opinion concerning the gods of the Painims.
[24] Herod., lib. i.

Chapter 3: Against the Gentiles and All Infidels

began (as man's natural corrupt inclination is too prone that way) to give honour and to do reverence to them; and not so contented, they proceeded further, and builded altars and temples to them, and at length consecrated priests, and appointed certain rites, ceremonies, and sacrifices, to be done there. The devil hereupon taking occasion and fit opportunity, (purposing always to seduce the world, and to hold them in error so far forth as he might) entered at last into those altars (which were dedicated to those men), and under the names of those men made way to have himself worshipped (instead of the true God). For true it is which the sacred Psalm witnesseth: "They sacrificed their sons and their daughters unto devils," (Psa. 106:37); and which Paul says, "The things which the Gentiles sacrifice, they sacrifice unto devils, and not to God," (1 Cor. 10:20): for the devils being entered into those altars, received their sacrifices offered to them, being glad they had them in such a predicament: and because their delusion should be the stronger, under the names of those men they would yield forth answers to such as came to demand any questions of them, and those their answers were written by their priests, and called oracles; and with such sleights those devilish spirits bewitched the world, and deceived them: of which, their oracles, more shall be spoken hereafter. But here first I make this argument against them: They which (howsoever ignorantly) worship devils, are far from the true religion; this is plain. But the Gentiles worshipped devils; *ergo, etc.* That the Gentiles worshipped devils (not God) may appear, first, by this reason, for that those their gods allowed (yea required) not beasts, but men to be sacrificed to them, delighting themselves in such infinite murders and manslaughters, as were most cruel and unnatural, signifying themselves to be thereby appeased, in which God is most displeased. For (as Polydore Virgil has collected[25]) the people of Rhodes sacrificed a man to Saturn. In the island Salamis a man was sacrificed to Agravala. To Diomedes in the temple of Pallas, a man was offered, who being thrice led about the altar by young men, was at last by the priest run through with a spear, and put into the fire and burnt. Among the people of Cyprus, Teucrus sacrificed human sacrifice to Jupiter, and left the same to posterity to follow. To Diana likewise human sacrifices were offered. The like was done to Hesus and Teutates. Amongst the Egyptians, three men a day which were sought out (if they were clean) were sacrificed to Juno. Amongst the Lacedemomans, they were accustomed to sacrifice a man to Mars. The Phoenicians, in the calamitous times of war and pestilence, were accustomed to sacrifice to Saturn their dearest friends. The people called Curetae sacrificed children to Saturn. At Laodicea a virgin was sacrificed to Pallas. And amongst the Arabians, every year a child was sacrificed, and buried under the altar. Also the Thracians, Scythians, the Carthaginians, and almost all the Grecians (especially when they were to go to war) sacrificed a man. All barbarous nations have done the like; yes, the Frenchmen and Germans; yes, the

---

[25] Polyd. De Inv., lib. v., cap. 8.

Chapter 3: Against the Gentiles and All Infidels

Romans themselves did the like sacrifice, as namely, to Saturn in Italy, a man was sacrificed at the altar; and not only so, but he was also to be cast down from a bridge into the river Tyber. Dionysius Halicamasseus writes, that Jupiter and Apollo were marvelous angry, for that the tenth part of men were not sacrificed to them, and therefore sought they revenge upon Italy.[26] Diodorus reporteth, that the Carthaginians when they were overcome of Agathocles King of the Sicilians, thought their gods to be angry with them; and therefore to appease them, sacrificed to them two hundred of the noblemen's sons at a time. O monstrous cruelty! Who then can possibly be persuaded otherwise, but that these gods of the Gentiles (which they thus worshipped and sacrificed to) *were mere devils*, considering that such monstrous, unkind, and unnatural slaughters of men (which must necessarily offend God the more) were the appeasements of their anger and wrath?

Again, these gods of the Gentiles were not only well-pleased with the sacrifices of the blood of men, but also well liked and allowed of fornication, adulteries, and all uncleanness; for at Alexandria the image of Saturn was most devoutly worshipped, whose priest, Tynannus by name, brought certain matrons of the city, which he had selected out to that image or idol, as being sent for by their god; and there when the lights were put out, had to do with them in the name of that their god. Also among the

---

[26] Dionys. Halic. in Antiq.

Nasamones it was the custom that the bride the first night after her marriage should lie with all the guests, in honour of the goddess Venus. I therefore conclude, that those gods of the Gentiles which delighted in the slaughter of men, and likewise in their filthiness and uncleanness, must necessarily be devils; for the kind and righteous God can abide none of these things, as any man's own reason, sense, and understanding may teach them.

2. Another argument to prove that the gods of the Gentiles were devils, is this,—Because the oracles which they gave forth in matters merely contingent, were either false, or else so ambiguous and uncertain, as that they were deceitful, and therefore could not come from God, but from the devil. This falsehood and deceitfulness of their oracles, Porphyry himself, the great patron of Paganism, testifies in a special book of the answers of the gods, in which he professes that he has gathered truly, without addition or detraction, the oracles that were most famous before his time with the false and uncertain event of it, in consideration of which event, he sets down his own judgment of their power in prediction after this manner: The gods do foretell some natural things to come, for that they observe the order of their natural causes; but in things which are contingent, or do depend upon man's will, they have but conjectures; only in that by their subtlety and celerity they prevent us; but yet they oftentimes lie, and deceive us in both kinds; for that as natural things are variable, so man's will is much more mutable. Thus far Porphyry of the prophecies of his gods; to which agrees

Chapter 3: Against the Gentiles and All Infidels

another heathen among the Grecians, named Oenomaus, who for that he had been much delighted with oracles, and more deceived, wrote also a, special book in the end of their falsehoods and lies; and yet shows, that in many things in which they were deceived, it was not easy to convince them of open falsehood, for that (cunningly) they would involve their answers (of purpose) with such obscurities, equivocations, amphibologies, and doubtfulness, as that always they would leave themselves a corner in which to save their credits. As for example, when Croesus, that famous and rich king of Lydia, consulted with the oracle of Apollo, whether he should make war against the Persians, and thereby obtain their empire? the oracle gave answer thus, *If Croesus without fear shall pass over Halys*, (which was a river that lay between him and Persia,) *he shall bring to confusion a great and rich kingdom*. Upon which words Croesus passed over his army, in hope to get Persia; but he lost Lydia his own kingdom, and was deceived by that uncertain oracle. Like answer gave the oracle of Apollo to Pyrrhus king of Epirus demanding whether he should prosper in the war against the Romans; for it was delivered in these words: *Aio te, Aeacida, Romanos vincere posse*;—I say that the son of Aeacus the Romans may overcome. Upon which oracle Pyrrhus the son of Aeacus thinking to be the conqueror, was himself vanquished by the Romans.

    A number more such oracles there were, wherewith the world was deceived, that trusted them; but I need not recite them; for (as it appears) the oracles and answers which their wicked spirits gave forth in matters future and merely contingent, were such as might be taken and construed two ways; and therefore their worshippers (if they had been wise to have noted their cunning and deceitful answers, containing no certainty at all) they had been as good never to come at them to inquire of any matter future; for they had such ambiguous answers, as by which they might remain as doubtful, and as unresolved as they were at first, and so depart home as wise as they came, or rather more fools than when they went. But what might be the reason why these devils, or devilish spirits, gave no certain answers to their worshippers in these matters future, whereof they were demanded? The reason is manifest; for no doubt they would if they could; that so their credit might have been the more. But it was a thing not in their power, but only reserved to God, to know and foretell certainly the things that are to come; for herein God provokes all the gods of the Gentiles to make trial and experience of their power, in these words, "Shew the things *(he says)* that are to come hereafter, that we may know that ye are gods," (Isa. 12:23): which shows that the certain foretelling of things future, manifests a Divine power, whereof these devilish spirits are not partakers; for had these wicked spirits such a power in them, as certainly to know and foretell such things as were to come, out of all doubt they would then have given such certain, plain, and undoubted oracles and answers in this behalf as would have purchased them everlasting credit in all the world. But now the falsehood and uncertainty and deceitfulness

Chapter 3: Against the Gentiles and All Infidels

of them have got them justly perpetual discredit in all the world, and manifested them to be no better than lying spirits, whose worshippers were miserably deluded by them; as even the heathen themselves have testified.

Having thus briefly, yet I trust sufficiently, disproved the religion of the Gentiles, as being a cruel, wicked, false, lying, and deceitful religion, having in it no certainty at all whereupon men might rest, or assure themselves; it remains now that I show and prove against them the truth of the Christian religion, which we profess. Where the first argument, to show the powerful and undoubted truth of it, shall be this, namely, the confession of the gods of the Gentiles, that is, of devils and hellish spirits themselves, who have given testimony of it, even to their own worshippers, especially when the time of Christ's appearing in the world (who should be the Light of the Gentiles) drew near and approached: for the manifestation whereof two oracles of Apollo may suffice; the one whereof was to a priest of his own that demanded him of true religion, and of God; to whom he answered thus in Greek: O thou unhappy priest! why dost thou ask me of God that is the Father of all things, and of this most renowned King's dear and only Son, and of the Spirit that contains all? *etc.* Alas! that Spirit will enforce me shortly to leave this habitation and place of oracles.[27] The other oracle was to Augustus Caesar, even about the very time that Christ was ready to appear in the flesh; for the said emperor now drawing to age, would needs go to Delphi,

---

[27] Suidas in Thulis; Porphyr. et Plut. De Oraculis.

and there learn of Apollo who should reign after him, and what should become of things when he was dead. Apollo for a great while would make no answer, notwithstanding Augustus had been very liberal in making the great sacrifice called *Hecatomb*; but in the end, when the emperor began to iterate his sacrifice, and to be instant for an answer, Apollo (as it were enforced to speak) uttered these strange words to him: An Hebrew child that rules over the blessed gods, commands me to leave this habitation, and out of hand to get me to hell. But yet do you depart in silence from our altars.[28] In this way it appears that this Hebrew child (which is our Christ Jesus) has power over the gods of the Gentiles, to command them to hell, from where they came, to enjoin them silence, and to remove them from their habitations; and therefore the religion of this powerful Jesus (of which He is the Author) must necessarily, even by the acknowledgment of the devils themselves (whom He commands) be the true religion.

    3. Another argument of the *Divinity* and *Truth* of it is this, namely, that it has removed by the puissant force of it all the gods of the Gentiles, in despite of them, ceased their oracles, and driven them clean out of the earth, so that now they are nowhere to be found. And so it was foretold by the Prophets, that Christ (when He came) *attenuabit omnes deos terra*,—shall wear out all the gods of the earth.[29] The truth whereof, all the world doth now see clearly to be certain and undoubted by the event. The

---

[28] Suidas in Vita Augusti; Niceph. Hist., lib, i, cap. 17.
[29] Soph. ii.

Chapter 3: Against the Gentiles and All Infidels

oracles and answers of these gods even in Cicero's time (as Cicero himself witnesseth,[30] who lived somewhat before the coming of Christ) began to cease; and at last by little and little they ceased altogether, and were utterly extinct. It is reported that in Egypt (when Christ was there with Joseph and His mother Mary) all the idols of that foolish and superstitious nation fell down of their own accord. Afterwards, in the time of the Emperor Adrian, all sacrifices to those gods ceased, as also the oracles of Apollo, and all other oracles became dumb. Wherefore Juvenal says, *Cessant oracula Delphis*, that is, the oracles cease at Delphi. And another poet says,—

> Excessere omnes adytis, arisque relictis,
> Dii, quibus imperium hoc steterat, *etc.* —Lucan.

That is, *All the gods by which this empire stood, have departed from their temples, and left their altars and place of their habitation.* Plutarch affirms the same,[31] and is much busied to search out the cause and reason of the ceasing of their oracles, who being a heathen was much troubled herewith, guessing at the matter, and vainly devising fond conceits in his brain, not able indeed to pierce into the very cause of it. But Porphyry (even that great patron of Paganism, and enemy of Christian religion) can teach him, or any other, the true cause of it, showing them that since the coming of Jesus their gods are dumb, and can do them no good, but

---

[30] Cicero De Divin., ii.
[31] Plutarch. De Defectu Oraculorum.

all are gone and departed from them. His words be these: *Nunc vero mirantur (inquit) si tam multos annos civitas peste vexetur, cum et Aesculapius et alii dii longe absint ab ea; postea enim quam Jesus colitur, nihil utilitatis a diis consequi possumus.* Now (he says) they marvel why this city is so many years vexed with pestilence, when as (indeed) Aesculapius and other gods be far gone and departed from it; for since the time that Jesus is worshipped, all our gods have been unprofitable to us. Considering then that Jesus (the Author of the Christian Religion) has silenced and utterly destroyed the gods of the Gentiles, (as histories and the visible event show,) His religion must necessarily be *the only true religion.*

4. What should I say more? even the Gentiles themselves, the most ancient, and the best, have testified of Jesus Christ, and of the truth of His religion; for, inasmuch as Christ was appointed before the creation of the world, to work the redemption both of the Jew and Gentile, and to make them both one people in the service of His Father; here hence it is that He was foretold, and not altogether unknown or unheard of to both these nations, and therefore divers forewarnings and significations of Him were left, as well among the Gentiles as the Jews, to stir them up to expect His coming. For, first by the consent of writers it is agreed,[32] that in those ancient times there were three famous men that lived together, namely, Abraham, (who, descending from Heber, was the father or

---

[32] Euseb. In Chro.

Chapter 3: Against the Gentiles and All Infidels

beginner of the Hebrews, who were afterward called the Jews,) and with him Job and Zoroastres, that were not of that lineage of Heber, but (as we call them for distinction sake) heathens or Gentiles. Job (we know) testifies of Christ, calling Him the Redeemer, and was most assured to see Him one day with his own eyes, and none other for him, although worms should destroy that body of his (as he himself testifies), (Job 19:25-27). Zoroastres living thus in Abraham's time also, might (by account of Scriptures) see or speak with Noah; for Abraham was born threescore years before Noah deceased; and hereof it is, that in the writings of Zoroastres, which are yet extant, or recorded by other authors in his name,[33] there be found very many plain speeches of the Son of God, whom he calls *secundam mentem*,—the second mind; but much more is to be seen in the writings of Hermes Trismegistus,[34] (who received his learning from this Zoroastres,) by whom appears, that these first heathen philosophers had manifest understanding of this second person in Trinity, whom Hermes calleth—The first begotten Son of God; His only Son, His dear, eternal, immutable, and incorruptible Son, whose sacred name is ineffable: so are his words; and after him again amongst the Graecians were Orpheus, Hesiodus, and others, that uttered the like speeches of the Son of God, as also did the Platonists, whose words and sentences were too long to repeat.

---

[33] Clem. Alex. Strom., lib. i.; Orig. Cont. Celsum, lib. vi.; Procl., lib. ii., 3; Parm., Plato.
[34] Herm. In Paeman., cap. i.

Moreover the Gentiles must remember, that they had also some Prophets among them, for Balaam was a Prophet among the Gentiles, and a Gentile, and he is such a one as testified of Christ, and of the star that should appear at His birth, (Num. 24:17); by means of whose prophecy it should seem the wise men in the East seeing that star, were assured that Christ was born, and therefore came a long journey to Judea to see Him, as one Gospel shows, (Matt. 2:1, 2). The same star is mentioned by divers heathen writers, as by Pliny under the name of a comet[35] (for so they term all extraordinary stars) which appeared in the latter days of Augustus Caesar, and was far different from all others that ever appeared. And Pliny says of it, *Is comita unus toto orbe colitur:*—That only comet is worshipped throughout all the world. Calcidius a Platonic says, that the Chaldean astronomers did gather by contemplation of this star, that some God descended from heaven to the benefit of mankind.[36]

The Gentiles also had certain women called Sybillse, which were Prophetesses, who being endued with a certain spirit of prophecy, uttered most wonderful particularities of Christ to come: one of them beginning her Greek metre in these very words, *Know thy God, which is the Son of God*. Another of them makes a whole discourse in Greek verse, called *Acrostichi*, expressly affirming in it, that Christ Jesus (by name) should be the Saviour, and that He was the Son of God, and expressly saying, that He should

---

[35] Plin., lib. ii., cap. 25.
[36] Calcid. apud Marsit. Picin. Tract. De Stella Mag.; Lact. contra Gent.

Chapter 3: Against the Gentiles and All Infidels

be incarnate of a Virgin, that He should suffer death for our sins, and that He should be crucified, that He should rise again, and be exalted into the glorious heavens, and from thence (at the time appointed) and at the day of the resurrection of all flesh, come again to the last judgment. Of these Sybils there were ten in number; and talking of His first coming into the world, they also say that *Rutilans eum sidus monstrabit*:—a blazing star shall declare Him.[37] These Sybils speak so plainly of Christ Jesus, as the Prophets among the Jews did, yes, more plainly, and as plainly as may be, and in a manner as fully as our Gospel speaks; and therefore if the Gentiles will believe their own Prophets, they must likewise believe the Christian religion (whereof Jesus Christ is the Author, of whom they abundantly testify).

Now, lest it might be thought by some suspicious heads, that Christians have devised and invented these things, as also that it may yet more fully appear, that Christ before His coming was notified over the world by means of those verses of the Sybils; it must be remembered, that Marcus Varro, a learned Roman, (who lived almost a hundred years before Christ,) makes mention at large of the Sybils,[38] (who in number, he says, were ten) and of their writings, countries, and ages, as also of the writers and authors that before his time had left memory of them; and both he and Fenestella (another heathen) do affirm, that the writings of the Sybils were gathered by the

---

[37] Sybil Samia, apud Betul.
[38] Varro, De Reb. Divin. ad Caesarem Pont. Max.

Romans from all parts of the world, where they might be heard of, and laid up with great diligence and reverence in the Capitol.[39] Sybilla Erythraea, who made the former acrostic verses, testifies of herself (as Constantine the Emperor records[40]) that she lived about six hundred years after the flood of Noah: and her countrymen Apollodorus Erythraeus and Varro do report that she lived before the war of Troy, and prophesied to the Grecians that went to that war, that Troy should be destroyed, (as it came to pass,) which was more than a thousand years before Christ was born. Cicero also (that died more than forty years before Christ was born) translated into Latin the former acrostic verses, (as Constantine says,) which translation was to be seen in his works, when Constantine wrote his Oration.[41] And finally Suetonius, an heathen, recordeth, that Augustus Caesar (before our Saviour Christ was born) had such special regard of the sayings of the Sybils, that he laid them up in more straiter order than before, under the altar of Apollo, in the hill Palatine, where no man might have the sight of them, but by special license.[42] And so much for the credit of the Sybils, who gave full testimony of our Saviour Jesus Christ (by name), and therefore if the Gentiles will believe them, (who were their own Prophets, and highly reverenced of all the world,) they must also believe our Gospel, and the Christian religion to be the only true religion.

---

[39] Fenest. De 15 Viris.
[40] See the Oration of Const. in Euseb. De Vit. Const., iv., 33.
[41] Cic. De Divinat., lib. ii.
[42] Sueton. De Vita, cap. iii.

Lastly, the Gentiles might have the understanding of Christ the Messiah by the Hebrew Scriptures, which were in the Greek language divers ages before Christ was born. For Ptolemy, King of Egypt, which had the famous library, was studiously inquisitive to search out the original of all nations and religions, and he found that the people of the Jews was the most ancient, and that they only had the most certain and undoubted history of the creation of the world; and therefore he sent to them, to send to him from Jerusalem seventy men, by whose help the sacred Bible might be translated out of Hebrew into their tongue, which was done accordingly. As also the Gentiles might have knowledge of this Messiah, either by access into the Jewish country, or by the access of the Jews into their country; as namely by their long bondage in Egypt, as also their long captivity in Babylon, *etc.* But I conclude this matter thus: since the Prophets of both Jews and Gentiles (that is to say, the Prophets of all the world) have given full, plain, and evident testimony of Jesus Christ, the Son of God, that therefore His religion is the only true religion, and all other to be rejected and detested.

5. That religion which is most ancient, is the true religion (for truth was first, insomuch as error is nothing else but the corruption of truth, or wandering from truth); but the religion whereof Christ is the Author, is the most ancient, inasmuch as Christ the Author of it is the most ancient of days, being the Son of God, as also because He is testified of by the Hebrew records, which are the most ancient writings in the world; *ergo*, the Christian religion

is that which must necessarily be the only true religion in the world: for it is a true saying of Tertullian, *Verum quod primum, quod posterius adulterium est.*—That is true, whatsoever is first: and that is adulterate which is not the first.[43] That the Hebrew records do testify and foreshow Christ to come, is declared before in the second chapter, and none can deny it: for He was promised to Adam, the first man that ever God made, under the name of the Seed of the woman, that should break the serpent's head; He was foretold to Abraham, that He should come of his seed, in whom all the nations of the earth should be blessed. Jacob foretold of Him, calling Him Shiloh, and that He should be the expectation of the Gentiles. God tells Moses of Him, and foreshows to him that He should be the Prophet whose voice all should hear and obey, *etc.* Considering, then, that He is come, and that He is the very same that was foretold by the writings of Moses, and by the Hebrew records, which are the most ancient records in the world, I conclude, that His religion, (whereof He is the Author) is *the only true religion.*

The antiquity of the Hebrew history to be long before all other, is acknowledged by the heathen themselves, and therefore I need not to prove it; only this I say, that Eupolemus and Eusebius also do say,[44] that letters (which are the beginning of words that should be written) were first found out by Moses, and by him delivered to the Jews, and that the Jews taught them to the

---

[43] Tertull. Contra Prax.
[44] Euseb. De Praepar. Evang., lib. x.

Chapter 3: Against the Gentiles and All Infidels

Phoenicians; and that lastly, the Grecians received them of the Phoenicians; and therefore the Hebrews must necessarily be they, amongst whom the first and most ancient records of the world were to be found, as Ptolemy also King of Egypt did find and affirm, and therefore made much of the Hebrew Scriptures. Now then forasmuch as the Hebrew Writings and Histories be the most ancient, they must also needs be supposed true, inasmuch as in themselves they all agree in a sweet harmony, and no other Records are able to disprove them; yes, if men will be so incredulous as to doubt of Moses' *History* because it is so ancient, why may they not (with as good reason also) doubt of any other history which is ancient, and long before their times? But because some are of so little belief, (although the History do sufficiently give credit to itself,) yet for better settling of their minds in this behalf, I will briefly show, that even the heathen historiographers and writers do confirm the same, that so the credit and reverence due to Moses may be reserved, and wicked tongues that bark against him may be stopped. The very heathen and profane writers themselves, that spoke of Moses, spoke of him most reverently; insomuch that Trebellius Pollio speaking of Moses, *solum Dei familiarem vocet:*—calls him the only man with whom God was familiar.[45] Cornelius Tacitus,[46] although he speaks what he can against the religion of the Jews, yet cannot discredit Moses' History, but is enforced to confess (according to

---

[45] Treb. Pol. in Claud.
[46] Tacit. Annal, lib. xxi.

the History written by Moses) that after there were blotches and swelling sores sent into the land of Egypt, which were noisome both to men and beasts, the King of Egypt then took order, that the people of the Hebrews should go out of his land, and depart whither they should be directed. Procopius also mentions Joshua, the son of Nun, Moses' successor, and says, that the people of Phoenicia, for fear of Joshua and the Israelites, left their own country, and departed into Africa: he mentions likewise the Jebusites, Gergashites, and the other people named in the sacred Bible. Orpheus, one of the most ancient writers next to Moses, and an heathen, mentions the two tables of stone in which the law of God was written, and wishes moreover all such as are studious of virtue to learn out of his verses Divine knowledge, by which (he says) they shall understand and know the Author of the world, which is one God, which created all things, cherishes all things, nourishes all things; who is not seen with mortal eyes, but is perceived only by the mind; which does no hurt to mortal men, insomuch as He is the Causer and Procurer of all good things. Furthermore, he addeth, That no natural man has seen God at any time, except only a certain most godly old man that came of the Chaldeans, (viz., Moses). At last he concluded with this saying,—That he had learned these things out of the monuments which God in times past had delivered in two tables of stone. Linus also says, that God created all things, and in the seventh day had finished all things. Homer also and Hesiodus testify the same, the one saying that the seventh day did perfect and finish all things; the other, *Septimam lucem fuisse sanctam et prcefulgidam:*—That the seventh day was most holy and bright. How the earth was without form before it was fashioned by God, Ovid testifies, calling it a *chaos*, which is *rudis indigestaque moles,*—a rude and unfashioned heap; which Homer and Hesiod also testify, calling it *Hyle,*—a certain unshapen and rude matter, which God afterwards brought into good form and fashion. These have testified, we see, of the creation of the world, (which is the great marvel of marvels,) affirming in manner the very words of Moses which he writes in Genesis, showing that the world had a beginning, and that God created heaven and earth, and all in it in seven days, and that the seventh day was holy to the Lord. And this truth of Moses' *History* concerning the creation of the world, all the chief and best learned philosophers amongst the heathens did also firmly believe. The flood that drowned the world, which we call the flood of Noah, not only Ovid testifies in his Metamorphosis, but also divers ancient heathen writers, namely, Berosus Chaldaeus, Hieronymus Aegyptus, Nicholaus Damascenus, Abydenus, and others, according as both Josephus and Eusebius do prove.[47] Concerning the tower of Babel, and confusion of tongues there, which Moses records Gen. 11, testimony is given by Abydenus, that lived about King Alexander's time, and by Sybilla, and by the words of Hestiaeus, concerning the land of Shinar, where it was builded; and

---

[47] Josephus De Ant. Jud.; Eusebius De Praep. Evang., lib. ix.

these Gentiles do show by reason, that if there had not been some such miracle in the division of tongues, no doubt but that all tongues being derived from one, (as all men are of one father) would still have retained the same language, which we see was seen long not to be in the world; the difference of languages in the world is a proof of that confusion of tongues.

Of the long life of the first Patriarchs, not only the forenamed Berosus Chaldaeus, Hieronymus Aegyptus, Nicholaus Damascenus, Abydenus, but also Msenetheus, that gathered the history of the Egyptians, Molus Hestiaeus, that wrote the Acts of the Phoenicians, Hesiodus, Hecataeus, Abderica Helanicus, Aeusilaus, and Ephorus, do testify, that these first inhabitants of the world did live so long. And they allege the reason of it to be for the multiplication of people, and for the bringing of all sciences to perfection, especially astronomy and astrology, which (as they write) could not be brought to any sufficient perfection by any one man that had lived less than six hundred years, in which space the great year (as they call it) returns about.

Of Abraham and his affairs, I have alleged from Heathen Writers before, as Berosus, Hecataeus, and Nicholaus Damascenus, but of all others, Polyhistor[48] alleges Eupolemus most at large of Abraham's being in Egypt, of his fight and victory in the behalf of Lot, of his entertainment by King Melchizedec, of his wife and sister Sarah, and of other his doings, especially of the sacrifice of

---

[48] Alex. Polyhist. De Judaica Historia.

Chapter 3: Against the Gentiles and All Infidels

his son Isaac. To whom agrees Melo in his books written against the Jews, and Artabanus, of the strange lake in which Sodom and Gomorrah were turned, by their destruction, called *Mare mortuum*—the Dead Sea, where nothing can live, both Galen, Pausanias, Solinus, Tacitus, and Strabo, do testify and show the particular wonders of it.[49] From Abraham down to Moses writes very particularly the said Alexander Polyhistor, albeit he mingles sometimes certain fables; by which it appears that he took not his story wholly out of the Bible. And he alleges one Leodemus, who (as he says) lived with Moses, and wrote the selfsame things as Moses did; and with these also do concur Theodorus a most ancient poet, Artabanus and Philon, Gentiles. And therefore it is manifest that Moses' *History* (as also all the rest of the Sacred and Canonical Scriptures) is no fable or feigned matter, (as the devil would make us believe,) but a true, certain, and most undoubted *History* in all points. All which matters be sufficiently and substantially shown also even by the heathen writings, which are too tedious to be here rehearsed.

But the great wonders and miracles which Moses did, being acknowledged to be done not by his own power, but by the power of God, do sufficiently give credit to him; of whom and of whose acts do bear witness, not only the fore-named, (especially Artabanus in his Book of the Jews,) but many others also, (especially Eupolemus,) out

---

[49] Galen. Be Simpl; Pans, in Eli; Solin. in Polyb.; Tacit. in lib. ult.

of whom Polyhistor recites very long narrations of the wonderful and strange things done by Moses in Egypt: yes, the miracles done by him, the greatest enemies that ever he had in the world, that is, Apion in his fourth Book against the Jews, and Porphyry in his fourth Book against the Christians,[50] do confess. And Porphyry adjoins more for proof of it, namely, that he found the same things confirmed by the story of one Sanchoniathon, a Gentile, who lived (as he says) at the same time with Moses: but all those miracles (say those two his great enemies) were done by art magic, and not by the power of God. But first, where could Moses, a simple shepherd, learn so much magic? Or why could not then the great magicians of Egypt either do the like, or at leastwise deliver themselves from those plagues that were in Egypt, especially since their study was in art magic from their infancy? Yes, why did they cry out, *This is the finger of God*, when they could not do as he did? (Exod. 8:19). Or let them answer, why Pharaoh King of Egypt did speak to Moses and Aaron, saying, "Intreat the Lord that He may take away the frogs from me, and from my people," (Exod. 8:8). His great magicians belike could not do it; yes, he signifies in that speech, that none can do it but God; yes, and that neither Moses nor Aaron could do it any otherwise than by praying to God. And indeed Moses and Aaron did by prayer to God effect it, at the very same time that the king did appoint it to be done; that he and all the world might know, that there was not any like to the God of Israel.

---

[50] Apion Contra Judaeos, lib. iv; Porph. Adversus Christian., lib. iv.

Where did you ever hear of such works done by art magic as Moses did when he divided the great and mighty Red Sea, that the people of Israel might go through the dry land? (Exod. 14:22); when the waters came together again upon Pharaoh and all his host, and drowned them, and all their glory in the sea? (Exod. 14:28); when he called so many quails upon the sudden into the camp, as sufficed to feed six hundred thousand men, besides women and children? (Exod. 16:13); when he made a very rock, by smiting it, to yield forth abundance of water, sufficient for the whole company of Israel? (Num. 20:11); when he caused the ground to open and swallow down alive three of the greatest of his army, Korah, Dathan, and Abiram, together with their tabernacles, bags, and baggages? (Num. 16:32).

Besides, what wondrous works or miracles soever Moses did, he always acknowledged to come from God, rejecting utterly all glory from himself, and attributing and yielding all the glory to God. Again, in his writings he Does not excuse nor conceal his own sin, nor the sin of his people, no, not the sin of Aaron his own brother, nor of Miriam his sister, nor of Levi his grandfather, nor of any other of his lineage and kindred. Neither did he once seek or go about (although he were in place of power and authority to do it) to bring in any of his own sons into the rule and government after his decease, (although he had many,) but left the only rule and government to a stranger, named Joshua, as God commanded. All which things do show (and many more too tedious to rehearse) that Moses, both in his writings, in his words, and in his works, was no man of ambition, or of worldly spirit; but a meek, humble, dutiful, obedient, and faithful servant of God in all matters.

The history of Moses, therefore, being the most ancient, and the same being most undoubted and certain true, insomuch as he and his history do plentifully testify of Christ which was to come, and should be heard in all that He should say and teach; it remains that His religion which He has taught to the world, is the only true religion, and all other religion (not grounded on the like antiquity and truth) to be abandoned.

6. None can discredit Moses, nor the Psalms, nor any of the Prophets amongst the Jews, but they must with this discredit Christ; for Christ says thus of Himself, "All things must be fulfilled which were written in the law of Moses, and in the Prophets, and in the Psalms," (Luke 24:44). Again, He sends such as would know of Him, whether He were the true Messiah, to the Scriptures of the Jews, saying in this way, "Search the Scriptures; for they are they which testify of Me," (John 5:39). So that Christ, Moses, the Psalms, and the Prophets, in a word, the whole Canonical Scriptures of the Jews do go arm-in-arm, and be linked together like inseparable friends that will not be sundered; and therefore the one is always a proof for the other, as likewise a disproof of the truth of the one is a disproof of the other; and therefore is it, that though the incredulous Jews be so false in friendship, as that they will not (through unbelief) take part with the Christians, yet the Christians be more firm, and will hold with the

Scriptures of the Jews to the death. Now if there were no more to prove the Divinity of Christ, but the great and wonderful miracles which He did, (some whereof were such as never any did before, nor could do, but God only,) it were sufficient to prove Him to be the Son of God, and that He came from the bosom of His Father. The great and many miracles that He did (being famous not only in Judea, but in all the Roman Empire, and so over all the world) are and were such as none of the heathen dare do, or can deny, but all acknowledge. And therefore I conclude, that the Christian religion, proceeding from so Divine a power, and from One whose works and wonders are above all the world, is the most undoubted true religion.

7. Christ did never any hurt on earth, but He did marvelous much good; He healed all manner of diseases; He caused the dumb to speak, the halt to go, the blind to see, and the deaf to hear; He stilled the raging of the winds and seas, gave sight to him that was born blind, raised the dead to life again, cast out devils, knew men's thoughts, and did such works as no man could do, except God were with him, yes, except Himself were God. Moreover, His life was such, as none was able to accuse Him of any sin, so pure and unreprovable was He. Again, the doctrine He taught was far from a worldly spirit, being most heavenly, most innocent, and most Divine, for never any man spoke as He spoke, nor with such authority. Again, He always pronounced that he sought not His own glory, (which deceivers are accustomed to do), but the glory of His Father; and as He spoke, so it was indeed. The whole

course of His life and death, resurrection and ascension, shows the same: for when the Jews would have made Him an earthly King, He would none of it, but conveyed Himself away, (John 6:15), teaching His ministers to do the like, (Luke 22:25, 26): for He proclaimed that His kingdom was not of this world, (John 18:36); but that He came to do the will of His Father. Over and above all this, He was the greatest Prophet that ever was, and foretold divers things, (as namely, that He should be crucified of the Jews, and the third day rise again; that Jerusalem and the temple should be destroyed ere that generation passed; that after His ascension, the Holy Ghost should come upon His disciples assembled at Jerusalem, and divers others,) all which, the world knows came to pass accordingly. And nothing which He has spoken, but it shall be performed; for there was never any fraud within His lips, or falsehood within His tongue. And therefore I conclude, that the religion of Him (who was most holy in His life, most harmless towards others, most bountiful towards all, most wonderful in His works, most true in His prophecies, most heavenly in His doctrine, not savoring of any carnal delight or worldly affection, nor by any way or means seeking His own glory, but the glory of God, and to do the will of His Father) is and must necessarily be the only true religion.

8. Another argument I frame thus: That religion which proceeds undoubtedly from God, *is the true religion.* But the Christian religion proceeds undoubtedly from God; *ergo, etc.* That it proceeds *undoubtedly* from God, I prove in this way: Either it must proceed from God, *or* from

the devil, *or* from men; but it is too holy to proceed either from men or devils; for it overthrow the works and kingdom of the one, and forbids the revenging spirit of the other, (commanding men to love their enemies, to do good to them that hate them, and persecute them) and it condemns their wanton eye, and the adulterous thoughts of their hearts, and their covetous humour, admitting no uncleanness or impurity, and forbidding all iniquity and wickedness, be it never so secret or close. Since, therefore, it is so opposite and contrary to men's affections, wherewith naturally they be carried, and that it commands to be holy, even as God is holy, it is manifest that it can neither be of man's devising, nor of the devil's invention: it remaineth, therefore, that it must necessarily be of God, and consequently the only true religion.

9. Another argument is this: That religion which respects only the glory of God, is, and must necessarily be, the only true religion. But such is the Christian religion; for it does not allow any man to glory in himself, but shows that whosoever glories, should glory in the Lord. (1 Cor. 1:30, 31; Rom. 4:2). Therefore the Christian religion is *the only true religion.*

10. Lastly, the spreading and prevailing of the Gospel of Christ over the universal world, when as all the world (both Jews and Gentiles) were set and opposed against it, demonstrates plentifully and effectually, that the Christian religion proceeds from God, and that God is the Author of it; for if it had not had a God to protect and patronage it, and to make it pass currently through the

world, it must necessarily have been utterly suppressed and choked, even in the springing and first rising of it: for after the ascension of Christ Jesus into heaven, what were His few Apostles (in the judgment of reasonable men) able to do, for the spreading and prevailing of it, against the force and power of all the world, which was then ready bent with all both fury and fraud, violence and vengeance, and with all their devices which they could invent to suppress it? or what eloquence had His few Apostles to persuade the world, or any in it, to the receiving and embracing of that Christian Religion, which they were appointed to preach? They (as all men know) were reputed and known to be unlearned men, but only that they were taught and instructed by the Spirit of God, which (according to the promise of Christ their Master) at the time appointed, descended down upon them, being assembled at Jerusalem; by which Spirit they were enabled to speak all languages, and emboldened to preach His Gospel and Religion in such sort, and with such puissant and Divine wisdom, none should be able to resist that Spirit they spoke by, howsoever their persons might be hindered, molested, vexed, and persecuted. This, even this is a wonder of wonders, and an infallible demonstration of the Divine virtue of the Christian Religion, that it having so few to publish it, and such as they were, and being encountered by all the princes and potentates of the world, it should notwithstanding so strangely prevail, as within a short time to be universally spread over the face of the whole earth! Who can now say but that it was protected,

Chapter 3: Against the Gentiles and All Infidels

and prevailed by the power of God, for the power of all the world was against it; and if the Christian religion had been no better protected by God, than by men, alas! it had perished long ago; yes, it had never lived until this day, but had been choked even at the first uprising, and as it were in the cradle or infancy of it. Let all wits therefore throw down themselves, and let all tongues freely confess the Divine virtue of the Christian religion, which could not be stopped nor suppressed; but was so mighty, as that the power of all the world, and all the devils in hell joining with them, was not able to stay the course and passage of it, but that it did prevail, and that within short space, over all the earth: and therefore the Christian religion (without all doubt) is *the only true religion*, which came down from heaven, being brought by Jesus Christ the true Messiah, from the bosom of God the Father. Of which (having so many and so infallible arguments to prove to every man's sense the truth of it) none can doubt, except he will also doubt whether the eye sees, the ear hears, and the heart understands the evidence of it is so clear and manifest, as that it is able, if not to convert, yet to convince all gainsayers whosoever, and to make us, that already profess, firmly to hold the same; knowing for certain that the Christian religion is the only true religion in the world, and that salvation is no where else to be sought: for run over all the religions of the world, and where shall you find any so pure, so Divine, so powerful, so miraculous? It has all the signs, tokens, arguments, and proofs that may be, for the splendent truth of it, and to demonstrate that undoubtedly *it came from God.*

CHAPTER 4: Islam: a False Religion

In which is Briefly Shown the Religion of Mahomet to be a False and Wicked Religion

If I shall speak something of the Mahometish religion, (Islam), I think the truth of the Christian religion will appear so much the more; for when black and white are laid together, the white carries the greater estimation and glory with it. And besides, Mahomet himself testifies of Christ, to be a great Prophet of God, and a great worker of miracles, and that the same Jesus Christ was born of the Virgin Mary, that He lived without sin among men; that He was a Prophet, and more than a Prophet, and that He ascended into the heavens: and therefore he reproves the Jews, for that they would not believe Him to be born of a Virgin. But on the other side, because he would not have Christ to bear credit above him, he disliked that he should be called or reputed the Son of God. But beside the testimony of all the former Prophets of the world, both Jews and Gentiles (as is before shown) do all teach, that he should be the Son of God. Suidas moreover confutes this false Prophet, who reports in his history that the Pharisees at Jerusalem called a council to find out the father of Jesus; they enjoined certain women to search His mother; the women affirmed they found her a Virgin; then was it recorded in the famous Register Book of the Temple,—

Jesus THE SON OF GOD AND OF MARY THE VIRGIN. This proves, not only that the Mother of Jesus was a Virgin, (which Mahomet truly held,) but also that Jesus was the Son of God (which Mahomet does not allow). And indeed Mahomet's religion is a *patched* religion, mixed partly with Judaism, partly with Gentilism, partly with Papism, partly with Christianism, being subtlely contrived for the erecting of the same, and to bring followers after him, whereof shall be spoken more hereafter.

The beginning of Mahomet's usurping, and of his sect, was thus:[51] Many hundred years after Christ, namely, in the year of our Lord 597, and in the reign of Mauritius the Emperor, when as Gregorius Magnus was Bishop of Rome, this Mahomet was born (being of the line of Ishmael the Son of Abraham, by Hagar the bond-woman, having to his father one Abdara, and to his mother one Emma, being very obscure and base parents) in Mecca a city of Arabia; his parents deceased, and left him a very young orphan, who in short time by misadventure was taken captive. This being once known to his kindred, one Ademonaples (Volateran says)[52] an Ishmaelite, bearing him good-will, for his favour and forwardness of wit, paid his ransom, and made him servant and factor in all his merchandize. Not long after his master died without issue, and his servant Mahomet matched with his mistress, a widow of fifty

---

[51] Matthaeus Par.; Maseus, Chron., lib. xiii.; Drenchsleer, Chron. de Saracen, et Turc. Orig.
[52] Volat., Georg., lib. xii.

years of age, called Eadigam, and (Paulus Diaconus says)[53] his own kinswoman; so that his master being of credit and substance, and his mistress (afterwards his wife) of no less account, and so shortly after departing this life, he succeeded them both in credit, and all their substance, and by this means grew to a great power and estimation. Diaconus further says, that this Mahomet, for the space of ten years, gave himself secretly by persuasion to bewitch the people, and other ten years after, with rogues and vagabonds that repaired to him, with force of arms, with sword, and shedding of blood, he spent in subduing of countries. And lastly, nine years he openly and manifestly enjoyed as a deceiver, a false prophet, and a king over those whom he had already infected throughout Arabia.

  Sabellicus writes,[54] that Mahomet's father was an heathen, and his mother an Ishmaelite; by which it came to pass, that whilst his mother taught somewhat of the religion of the Hebrews, and his father on the other side the religion of the Gentiles, Mahomet (like a dutiful child, but not like a discreet son) obeyed both, and that was some cause of the mixed and patched religion. He had the falling sickness, which took him so extremely, that he grovelled along the ground, and foamed piteously at his mouth. His wife being of great honour and substance, bewailed her hard hap in matching with a beggarly rascal, and a diseased creature; but he (with his wily companions) having taught a dove to feed at his ear, in which he had put

---

[53] Paul. Diac., Res. Rom., lib. xviii.
[54] Sabel., Aenead. viii., lib. viii.

grains of corn, persuaded his wife to be content, and that he was another manner of man than she took him to be; namely, that he was a prophet, that the Spirit of God fell upon him, and that the angel Gabriel in the form of a dove came to his ear, and revealed to him secrets from God, whose presence he was not able to abide; and therefore was it that he so prostrated himself, and lay in a trance. His wife being herewith satisfied, she began to chat the same amongst her gossips, saying, *Say nothing, my husband is a prophet.* The women after their manner (whereof some of them can keep no counsel) blazed abroad that Mahomet was a prophet, and so from women it came to men.

  This being once noised, they flocked to him from all parts of Arabia.[55] He being thoroughly instructed in Satan's school, and well seen in magic, observed the present opportunity. The Romans and Persians then warring together, Mahomet with his Arabians went, and first took part with the Romans; but afterwards served them a sly touch, and forsook them, and thereby weakened that side. In a while after he espied the Persians go to wrack, and having despised the Romans, he sets less by the Persians,[56] and then sets forth himself with might and main, with his captains and lieutenants (called Amirel) to subdue nations, and to destroy the Christians, to the end that he might establish that false religion devised by himself, and his wicked confederates. He prevailed wonderfully, and in short time after his decease (in the

---

[55] Aventin., Annal., lib. iii.
[56] Zonaras, Annal., tom. iii.

Chapter 4: The False Religion of Islam

time of Ebubezer and Haumer, that successively reigned after him in Arabia) there were got and subdued to the Arabians, the region of Gaza, the city of Bostra in Arabia, Damascus, Phoenicia, Egypt, Palestina, the city Jerusalem, all Syria, Antioch, Edessa, Mesopotamia, all Persia; yes, and, in a manner, all Asia. But I may not forget the end of Mahomet, who in an evening sitting up late in his. palace, and having taken his fill of wine, in which one of his companions had poured some poison, felt his accustomed sickness approaching, and made haste forth, saying, he must necessarily depart to confer with the angel Gabriel, and go aside, lest his glorious presence should be an occasion of their deaths; forth he went, and remembering that a soft place was best for his falling sickness, down he fell upon a dunghill, groveling along with great pain, foaming at the mouth, and gnashing his teeth; the swine came about the dunghill, fell upon him, wounded him sore, and had eaten him up, had not his wife and others of his house heard the noise of the hogs, and rescued the false prophet. Antoninus reporteth,[57] that he was not without sundry diseases, which intemperate diet brought to him; namely, the pleurisy, and a kind of lethargy; for oftentimes his senses seemed to be taken from him. He continued drooping the space of fourteen days; at length he departed this life. His belly had such a swelling that it seemed ready to burst, and his little finger bowed backwards. In the time of his sickness he commanded them that were about him, that when breath departed his body, they should not

---

[57] Ant., Chron., par. ii., tit. 13, cap. 5.

straightway bury him; for he said, that within three days he would ascend into heaven; but hereby appeared that he was a false prophet, for they kept him above the ground the third and fourth day, yea (as *Flores Historiarum* testifies) the space of thirty days, in great hope he would rise, and ascend according to promise; but they saw nothing, saving that they felt an intolerable stench, so that in great disdain (Antoninus says) *Eum longe a dominus projecerunt*,—they cast him far from houses. But his companions, (such as consulted with him, and concealed his falsehood and treachery,) remembering themselves, and judging that the disdain of Mahomet would be their discredit, and his fall their foil and shame, they fetched him again, they chest him in an iron coffin (Sabellicus and Nauclerus says);[58] they bring him to the famous temple of Mecca (in which city he was born) with great solemnity, as if he had never been seated upon the dunghill with swine; they convey to the roof of the temple mighty loadstones; they lift up the iron coffin, where the loadstones, according to their nature, draw to them the iron, and hold it up, and there hangs Mahomet on high!

Those that embrace the religion of Mahomet, are called Saracens,[59] for it was the pride of Mahomet to have them so called, to advance his own doctrine and profession, because he knew himself lineally descended of Ishmael the son of Hagar the bond-woman; therefore to

---

[58] Sabel., Aenead. viii. lib. vi.: This was the report of old, Anton., Chron., par. ii., cap. 5; Wolfang.; Drenster., Chron.; Naucl., Gen., 22.
[59] Sabel., Aenead. viii. lib. vi.

Chapter 4: The False Religion of Islam

avoid this reproach, he bare the world, that he came of Sarah the free-woman, the wife of Abraham, and called himself and his followers Saracens. Sabellicus writes,[60] that the Grecians of spite are accustomed to call the Saracens, Hagarenes; for that they came not of Sarah, but of Hagar.

This Mahomet, while he lived, used the company of Christians, Jews, and Infidels: *Et ut popularior esset ejus lex, ex omnium gentium sectis aliquid assumpsit*: And to the end his law might be the more favoured, he borrowed something of every sect. Satan furnished him with three instruments, as helps to bring his mischievous intent about. The first was a Jew, a great astronomer, and a magician, who opened to him at large the Jewish follies; the second, one John of Antioch; the third, one Sergius a monk, both abominable heretics. Every one played his part. To flatter the Christians, he was content to be baptized of Sergius;[61] and of these heretics, he learned with the Sabellians to deny the Trinity; with the Manichees to establish two beginnings; with Eunomius to deny the equal power of the Father and the Son; with Macedonius to call the Holy Ghost a creature; and with the Nicolaites, to allow many wives, and wanton lust. Sergius the monk also persuaded Mahomet in his Alcoran (so is the book of the law termed as the *Koran*) to commend the humility of Christian monks and priests;[62] he made him also deliver the Sacracens a

---

[60] Sabel., Aenead. viii. lib. vi.
[61] Ibid.
[62] Ant., Chro., par. ii., tit. 15, cap. 2.

monk's cowl, which they use to this day, also instar *monachorum multas genuflexiones*,—many duckings and crouchings like the monks. Matthias a Michovia addeth[63] that they use shaving, and this no doubt was the monks' doctrine. They commend the blessed Virgin Mary,[64] confess God to be the Governor of all things, and that Jesus Christ was the Apostle of God, begotten by the angel Gabriel on Mary the Virgin, who never knew man, and that He was greater and worthier than man. They allow the miracles that Christ did,[65] and the Gospel, (so far forth as it agrees with the Alcoran) and Moses, and the Old Testament, correcting in it (so presumptuous is the spirit) certain errors. He called himself a prophet, and that he was sent of God to supply the imperfections of all laws. He forbad his followers all pictures and images in their temples. He forbad the eating of swine's flesh. He commanded purifyings and washings, *ad similitudinem Judaorum*,—after the manner of the Jews. The Christians have Sunday for their Sabbath, the Jews Saturday, and Mahomet Friday, to dissent from the Hebrews and Christians; or, as Antoninus writes, in the honour of Venus the goddess of Arabia, thereby the rather to win that country people. And thus it pleased him to devise a religion mixed of all these, to the end he might have of all religions some to build up his kingdom. And indeed Mahomet took the advantage of the time; for that time was a time of

---

[63] Matthias a Michov. De Sarmat.
[64] Asian., lib. i., l. 7; Laonic. de Ture., lib. iii.
[65] Sabel., Aenead. viii. lib. vi.

dissension among princes, and of division amongst those which called themselves Christians. Heraclius the Emperor, and Chosroes King of Persia, were at deadly enmity, one warring against another. The Scythian nation were of neither side, but at last against both, raising a power of themselves, having Mahomet their ring-leader. The Church was troubled with divers sects and heresies, as with Nestorians, Jacobites, Monothelites, *etc.* And then was there contention amongst the bishops who should have the proud title of universal bishop. God was highly displeased with this wickedness, and suffered nations to rise as a rod or scourge to whip His people; for where the hedge is broken, there it is easy for the beasts of the field to enter and spoil.

Now the vanity and falsehood of this religion may be proved thus:

First, By the newness of it; for it is but of late years begun, and there was never any prophecy that did allow of such a prophet, or of the doctrine of such a one. And therefore he comes in his own name, and so consequently not to be received.

Secondly, He did no miracle at his coming, and therefore no reason that any should believe in him. He spoke to the Saracens of himself: *Non sum miraculis aut indiciis ad vos missus;*—I am not sent to you with miracles and signs.[66] There was no Divine power shown in all his practice.

---

[66] Matth. Paris, Hist. Aug. in Hen. III.

Thirdly, It is manifest that Mahomet was a false prophet,[67] because he said, That within three days after his death he should ascend into heaven, which was notoriously false, as before appears.

Fourthly, The religion of Mahomet is fleshly, consisting in natural delights and corporeal pleasures; [68]which show that man, and not the Divine Spirit of God, is the author of it, for it is permitted the Saracens by that his law to have four wives, (though these be of nigh kin,) yea five, marrying them virgins; and to take besides as many of them which they have bought and taken captives, as their ability will serve to maintain. The paradise likewise promised to his followers is this,[69] namely, They shall have garments of silk, with all sorts of colors, bracelets of gold and amber, parlors and banqueting-houses upon floods and rivers, vessels of gold and silver, angels serving them, bringing in gold, milk, silver, wine, lodgings furnished, cushions, pillows, and down beds, most beautiful women to accompany them, maidens and virgins with twinkling eyes, gardens and orchards, with arbors, fountains, springs, and all manner of pleasant fruit, rivers of milk, honey, and spiced wine; all manner of sweet odors, perfumes, and fragrant scents; and to be short, whatsoever the flesh shall desire to eat. Thus fleshly people have a fleshly religion, and a fleshly paradise to inhabit. But like prophet, like people, and like religion; for Mahomet

---

[67] Flor. Hist.
[68] Jacob de Vor., Legend 157; Laonic. De Reb. Turc., lib. iii.
[69] Ant., Chron.

Chapter 4: The False Religion of Islam

himself was such a fleshly fellow, as that though modest ears are loathe to hear, yet because the filthiness of this prophet may not be concealed, I must utter it. He committed a *bestial* crime: Bonfinius writes it.[70] Again, he committed adultery with another man's wife, that upon displeasure was from her husband; and when he perceived the murmur of the people, he feigned that he had received a paper from heaven, in which it was permitted him so to do, to the end he might beget prophets, and worthy men. Again, Mahomet (as Caelius reporteth)[71] had forty wives; and further he gloried of himself, that it was given him from above to exceed ten men, (Cleonard says,)[72] fifty men, (Antoninus says,[73]) in carnal lust and venery. Avicenna[74] one of Mahomet's own sect, is himself brought in disliking of this religion, for this reason: Because Mahomet (he says) has given us a law, which shows the perfection of felicity to consist in those things which concern the body: whereas the wise and sages of old had a greater desire to express the felicity of the soul than of the body; as for the bodily felicity, though it were granted them, yet they regarded not, neither esteemed it, in comparison of the felicity which the soul requireth. His paradise and doctrine is such, as there seems small difference between Epicurism, Atheism, and Mahometism.

---

[70] Bonfin., lib. viii.; Bernard, in Rosar., part i., serm. 14; Ant., Chro., par iii., tit. 15, cap. 2.
[71] Caelius Nichol.
[72] Cleon., Epist. 1.
[73] Antonin., Chron., par. ii., cap. 5.
[74] Avicenna, Metaphys.

Fifthly, Mahomet's law is a tyrannical law, for he made it death to dispute of it, and if any man speak against it (he says) *Proditore occidatur*:—Let him be traitorously put to death.[75] And again, *Sine audientia occidatur*:—Let him be put to death without coming to his answer.[76] *Qua sanctione* (Sabellicus says[77]) *palam fecit nihil sinceri in ea lege esse, etc.* By which decree he manifested, that there is nothing sincere in that law, *etc.* Moreover he wrote in the Arabian tongue, and taught his followers, that his religion *A gladio caepit, per gladium tenetur, et in gladio terminator*,—Began by the sword, is holden by the sword, and is finished or ended in the sword:[78] which shows that the sword and arm of flesh is all the author and protector that his religion has. Again, Mahomet made this law amongst them, saying, "He that slayeth his enemy, or is slain of his enemy, let him enter and possess paradise." He spoke like a man with a carnal spirit; teaching revenge to the uttermost, and promising paradise to such; but no proof of a Divine spirit appears in him.

Sixthly, As Mahomet's religion is defended by force of sword and fraud, insomuch as he made it death to call it into question; so likewise did it begin, as by the force of sword, so likewise by notable fraud, and was established through wiles, deceit, subtlety, and lies: for first he having the falling sickness, persuaded his wife and others, that it was the power of God, and the presence of the angel

---

[75] Anton., Chron., par. ii., tit. 13, cap. 4.
[76] Sabel., ut supra.
[77] Matth. Paris, Hist. Aug., in Hen. III.
[78] Paul. Diac., Res Rom., lib. xviii.

Chapter 4: The False Religion of Islam

Gabriel, that caused him to fall down. Sergius the heretical monk was at hand, and bare false witness to the same (Zonaras says).[79] He told them that the same dove which he taught to feed at his ear, was sometimes an angel, and sometimes the Holy Ghost. He had three companions ail of a confederacy, to devise and face out lies with him. When he perceived that men gave ear to him, he feigned that the angel Gabriel had carried him to Jerusalem, and thence to have lifted him up to heaven, and there to have learned his law. He made the Saracens believe, that before God made the world, there was written in the throne of God, There is no God, but the God of Mahomet.[80] When he had framed his Alcoran,[81] and bound it up fair, he caused secretly a wild ass to be taken, and the book to be bound about his neck, and as he preached to the people, upon a sudden he stood amazed, as if some great secrecy was revealed to him from above, and brake out, and told the people, Behold, God has sent you a law from heaven; go to such a desert, there you shall find an ass, and a book tied about his neck. The people ran in great haste, they found it so as he had said, they take the ass, they bring the book, they honour the prophet.[82] Touching divorced and separated wives, he told the Saracens that he had received a paper from heaven. He used soothsaying and divination, the which at Fessa, a city of Mauritania, to this day is called Zarragia. He

---

[79] Zonaras, Annal., tom. iii.
[80] Ant., Chro., par. viii., tit. 13, cap. 5.
[81] The *Koran*-Editor's Note.
[82] Avirus, lib. ii., cap. 12; Joh. Leo, lib. iii., cap. 23; Aphric.; Bern, in Rosar., part i., serm. 10.

persuaded his followers, that at the end of the world he should be transformed in the form of a mighty ram, full of locks and long fleeces of wool; and that all that held of his law, should be as fleas shrouding themselves in his fleeces, and that he would jump into heaven, and so convey them all thither. These and such like were his flights, to beguile a foolish, rude, and barbarous country people; the foolery, pride and vanity of whose religion, I trust, everyone sufficiently perceives.

Seventhly, Mahomet's religion is no true religion, but a mere device of his own, and of three others his false conspirators; for he has patched together his Alcoran of the doctrine of Heathens, Indians, and Arabians, of superstitious Jews, of Rechabites, of false Christians and heretics, as Nestorians, Sabellians, Manichees, Arians, Cerinthians, Macedonians, Eunomians, and Nicolaites, of illusions, and inventions of their own; and lastly, (for further credit,) he borrowed some out of the Old and New Testament. But God will not thus be served; for He delivered His mind of old to Israel, and He is not changed, but continues the same God still. "Ye shall not (God says) do whatsoever is right in your own eyes. What thing soever I command you, observe to do it: thou shalt not add thereto, nor diminish from it," (Deut. 12:8, 32). Satan being conjured to deliver the truth of the Alcoran of Mahomet, said, that in it were comprised twelve thousand lies, and the rest was truth;[83] by all likelihood very little. And therefore I conclude, that there is no evidence to prove

---

[83] Fascicul. Temp.

Chapter 4: The False Religion of Islam

Mahomet a true prophet; many prove him to be a false prophet, and blasphemous, and presumptuous, and his religion to be a wicked, carnal, absurd, and false religion, proceeding from a proud spirit, and human, subtle, and corrupt invention, and even from the devil, the crafty father of lies, a murderer, and man-killer from the beginning. And so much hereof may suffice.

CHAPTER 5: Roman Catholicism is the Apostate Church and Antichrist

In which is Shown that the Church of Rome is Not the True Church of God, Nor Observes the True Religion

I am now entering into that great controversy between the Protestants and the Papists, whether of them should be the true Church, and true worshippers of God in Christ; for they both acknowledge God, and Christ His Son; and all the Sacred and Canonical Books of the Scriptures, they confess to come from God, and from His Divine Spirit, as indeed they could come from no other. But whiles they both confess this Book, it is good reason that they should both stand to the arbitrement and judgment of these Books, for the trial of the true Church; which if they do, (as indeed they must,) this controversy is at an end, and not worthy to be made a question, or to be doubted of; for by the Sacred and Canonical Writings it shall by-and-by be manifest, that the Church of Rome cannot be the true Church possibly. But first let us hear what it says for itself, and what good grounds it has for the fortification of it. For if it be not built on a good foundation, and upon such grounds as will hold, the whole building is like to lie in the dust, and to come to ruin.

1. They hold very stiffly (but not so strongly) that the Church of God militant here upon earth, is visible to

the outward eye, and may be pointed out by the finger at all times, in such sort as that one may know whither to resort, as to the congregation of God's people, there to join himself to them, and to praise and pray to God with them, and to do those things that He requires at their hands. But all this cannot profit them, nor hurt us; for as in the Primitive Churches persecuted by those tyrannical and heathen emperors, there was a Church of God (though not seen of them) who had their meetings and assemblies amongst themselves (though secretly because of their enemies); so likewise in the days of Queen Mary, as also in all other times of the persecution of our Church by the Romish Bishops and their partakers, our Church no doubt was, and might be; and they likewise had their meetings and assemblies, though both they and the place of their resort were unknown to those their persecutors.

In the time of Dioclesian the emperor (especially) Christians were so wasted, as to the judgment of men none were remaining; their books were burned, the churches destroyed, and themselves put to death. In the end when this great havoc was made, and cruelty had wasted and destroyed all that could be found, where was then the visible Church? It must necessarily be then enforced to hide itself; and so it was, and the glory of it so eclipsed, that for a while it shined nowhere. And therefore the Church is not always visible and seen to the outward eye, nor splendent in the faces and sight of men, and yet a true Church notwithstanding, as then it was; for it is the sun, though it be sometimes overwhelmed with a cloud; and it is fire still, though it be sometimes raked up in embers; and so the true Church is and may be, although not seen or known to the world; yes, though it seem overwhelmed with tyrannical malice, and hide itself as though it were clean extinct.

Let them tell me where the Church was visible, when being assembled at Jerusalem, there arose a great persecution against it, insomuch as they were all dispersed and scattered, as the text shows? (Acts 8:1). Or let them tell me, where or how the Church was visible when Christ was smitten, and all the rest were scattered and hid, and concealed themselves; the face of the visible Church was then not in Christ and His Apostles, but in the Jews among the Scribes and Pharisees: and therefore if visibility be such a mark of the true Church, then these who crucified Christ were the true Church, and not Jesus Christ and His Apostles; which who dare affirm? yes, who will not deny? yes, when the Shepherd was smitten, and the sheep scattered, and yet a true Church, who can deny but that a true Church may be, though it be not apparently visible, and seen to the world? What shall I say more? Does not St. John in his Revelation testify expressly, that the Church of Christ (signified there by a woman) *fugit in solitudinem,*— fled into a desert, or wilderness, where she had a place prepared for her of God, and where she could not for a certain season be found of her persecutors? (Rev. 12:6). Let them further show me how the Church was visible in the time of Elijah the Prophet, when he complained that he himself was left alone. "O Lord, (said he,) they have forsaken Thy covenant, thrown down Thine altars, and slain Thy Prophets with the sword; and I, even I only, am left," (1 Kings 19:10). Elijah did not think himself to be *solus Propheta relictus*, (as Campan answered in the Tower); I say he spoke not of himself only in that respect; but in this respect, that he took himself to be the only true worshipper that was left in Israel; which is manifest by the answer which God gave him, namely, that besides him He had seven thousand true worshippers yet remaining, which had not bowed their knee to Baal. I demand of the Papists, when Elijah knew no other true worshipper of God but himself, how the Church was visible? for whither he should go to find a true worshipper, he knew not. Again, it is written in 2 Kings 16, that under the reign of Ahaz, there was taken a pattern of the altar of the idolaters of Damascus, and that Urijah the high priest removed the altar of the Lord, (verses 10, 11); by which it appears, that the priesthood was corrupted, the altar removed, and consequently the sacrifices ceased, *etc*. What visibility of the true Church could there be in those days, either of Ahaz, Manasseh, and other kings being idolaters, when the Temple itself (where only, by the law of God, the Jews were to offer the sacrifices) was polluted and defiled with heathenish idolatry? What Church or congregation could any man (in this case) have resorted to, to have performed a true and acceptable sacrifice to God in those times, when the temple of Jerusalem (which was the place to worship at) would admit no true worshippers, but only idolaters? It is therefore manifest that a true Church may be, thought they does not know a congregation of God to resort to; yes, thought it be close and not seen or known one to the other, nor yet to the world. And consequently visibility (which the Papists make a mark of the Church) is no perpetual mark of it. Yes, if such visibility should be a mark of the true Church, then were the idolatrous people in the time of Elijah, in the time of Ahaz, Manasseh, and many other Kings of Israel that were idolaters, the true Church, who indeed were the false Church; and then were Elijah and all other the true worshippers of God, who had in those times no places left to sacrifice in, the false Church, which is absurd. Chrysostom says, that in the time of the abomination of desolation (spoken of by Christ Jesus, in Matt. 24). that is, in the time of wicked heresy, which is the army of Antichrist, (as he expounds it,) *Nulla probatio potest esse Christianitatis, neque effugium potest esse Christianorum aliud volentium cognoscere fidei veritatem, nisi Scripturae Divince*: —No proof can be made of Christianity, neither can there be any other refuge for Christians, which are desirous to know the true faith, but only the Divine Scriptures.[84] And therefore I conclude (which is apparent) that the true Church sometime is in such a state, as that visibleness cannot discern or prove it, but only the Divine Scriptures must demonstrate and declare it; and consequently it is demonstratively manifest, that it is no true position of the Papists, *That the Church of God is always and evermore visible, seen, and splendent, to the outward eye and view of the world.*

---

[84] Chrys. in Mat. 24.

Chapter 5: The False Religion of the Church of Rome

Wherefore the Papists do us great injury, and bewray their own ignorance, when they would have us to show our Church in all times and ages (which notwithstanding perhaps may be done); for our Church was always, though it were not seen or known to them, but lay hid and kept itself close from their fury and tyranny, as the first and primitive Churches did from their bloody persecutors. Our Church was then persecuted in those times when it could not be seen, and many then, like constant martyrs, endured the tyranny of that Romish Religion; so that some were banished, others fled into other nations, some endured martyrdom at home, some others hide themselves, but the whole Church generally was vexed and oppressed. And therefore when our Church was thus persecuted, it is a good argument (I think) to say: We had our Church then and always, though a persecuted Church, though a Church chased and pursued, though a Church scattered, though a Church not seen or visible to them, yes, though in itself it were enlightened from God many ages together, namely, till the tyranny of Antichrist were over-past.

    2. Another erroneous position by which they are miserably deceived, is this, *They hold the Church cannot err*; and therefore suppose, because the Church of Rome was once the true Church of God, therefore it is so now and evermore. As though there might not be an apostasy in the Church, which St. Paul affirms there should, (2 Thes. 2:3, 4); or as though a particular Church (for the Church of Rome is but a particular Church) could not err; yes, as though general councils (which represent the whole

Church) could not err; for so they affirm, but how truly let the world judge. And if it may be shown that general councils have erred, or may err, then they yield their cause in this behalf. I wish they would for their own sakes; for false Jesuits and Seminaries do but deceive themselves and others, to their own confusion in this world, and, except they repent, in the world to come.

That general councils may err, is manifest by Augustine, who plainly teacheth, that only the Scriptures cannot err, all other writers may err, provincial councils may err.[85] Lastly, he says, *Concilia quae fiunt ex universo orbe Christiano priora posterioribus saepe emendari, cum aliquo experimento rerum aperitur quod clausum erat, et cognoscitur quod latebat:*—That general councils which are gathered of all the Christian world, are often corrected, the former by the latter, when, by any trial of things, that is opened which was shut, and that is known which was hidden. A general council may be corrected (Augustine says); *ergo*, it may err. And therefore Augustine speaks plainly to Maximinian the Bishop of the Arians,[86] Neither ought I to allege the Council of Nice, nor thou the Council of Arimine, to take advantage thereby; for neither am I bound nor held by the authority of this, nor thou of that; set matter with matter, cause with cause, or reason with reason; try the matter by the authority of the Scriptures, not proper witnesses to any of us, but indifferent witnesses to us both.

In the time of Constantine, that Christian

---

[85] August., tom. vi., Contra Donatist., lib. ii.
[86] Aug. Con. Maximin., lib. iii., cap. 8.

Chapter 5: The False Religion of the Church of Rome

Emperor, was the first and last Council of Nice, in which according to our Creed was decreed, that Christ was God, as well as man. In the time of Constantius (Constantinus's son) favoring the error of the Arians, it was decreed in the Council of Arimine, that Christ was not God, but man. This Council of Arimine did err (and that grossly) in a matter of faith. *Ergo*, it is palpable that a general council may err, even in matters of faith.

Again, general councils have been contrary one to the other, and that in matters of faith; as the Council of Constantinople condemned the setting up of images in the Church, and the Council of Nice afterward allowed images. One of them (being contrary) must necessarily be erroneous; *ergo*, a general council may err.

The general council confesses itself that it may err:[87] for the whole council prays in the end of a general council (in a set form of prayer, that is appointed to be said after every council) namely, that God would *Ignorantics ipsorum par cere, et errori indulgere;*—Spare their ignorance, and pardon their error. *Ergo*, a general council may err.

The Pope of Rome (whom the Papists hold for head of their Church) may err; *ergo*, their whole Church may err. Augustine proves it errs. *Beatae memories Innocentius Papa sine baptismo Christi, et sine participatione corporis et sanguinis Christi, vitam non habere parvulos docet:*[88]—Behold, Pope Innocentius of blessed memory teaches, that young children cannot be

---

[87] Concil., tom. i., De Ord. Celeb. Concil.
[88] Lib. ii. ad Bonif. contra Epist. Pelag., cap. 4.

saved, except they receive the baptism of Christ, and also the communion of the body and blood of Christ. But this is taxed for an error; *ergo*, the Pope of Rome may err, and consequently the whole Church under him, except perchance members have a privilege above the head. But what shall I need to stand hereupon? their own canon law (as it is evident in the decrees)[89] says expressly, that if the Pope be found negligent of his own and his brethren's salvation; yes, though he lead innumerable people by heaps to the devil of hell, no mortal man may presume to reprove him, because he himself being to judge all, is to be judged of none, *nisi deprehendatur a fide devius*:—Except he be found erring from the faith: by which it appears, that they thought he might err in matters of faith, or else that exception was put in vain. But the Pope is no other than a man, as also the members of his Church be, and *Humanum est errare*:—All men are subject to error. Let every man take heed how he trusts the Pope or any man mortal; for it is written, (Jer. 17,) *Maledictus harm qui in homine confidit*:— "Cursed is the man that putteth his trust in man," (verse 5). And why? Because (as the Prophet David says, (Psa. 116,) "All men are liars," (verse 11). But when the doctrine of that man of Rome, and of his Church is in divers things clean contrary to the express Word of God, who can deny but it is an apparent erring Church? As when it established ignorance to be the mother of devotion, which Christ calls the mother of error, saying, "Ye do err, not knowing the

---

[89] Part i., dist. 40, cap. Si Papa.

Scriptures," (Matt. 22:29). Who can choose but think that it has no good meaning in it, but purposed only to build up the pride of the Pope, of his cardinals, bishops, priests, monks, and other their ecclesiastical men? Christ bids the people to "search the Scriptures," (John 5:39); this Antichrist forbids them, saying, it is perilous, it causes schisms, sects, and heresies, as though they were wiser than Christ. Again, the Apostle Paul commands that the Word of Christ should dwell plentifully in the people, by which they might teach themselves, (Col. 3:19). But the Pope of Rome, and his Church, does not allow plentiful knowledge of the Word in them; yes, ignorance is the knowledge that he would desire them to have. Who would not justly suspect such a Church, and such a religion, yes, condemn it, when to maintain and continue their Church in errors, they would have none of the people to search any Scriptures, by which they might be discovered? Thus the silly Papists (whom I pity) are led like blind men they does not know whither, and with their *implicita fides* (which is to believe for their part they does not know what) are lamentably seduced. It is good themselves should see and know what they believe, and that their faith and belief be right, lest at last they be (through overmuch trust of their teachers) extremely deceived. The people of Berea were highly commended, and it is noted to their praise, that they searched the Scriptures, to see whether those things were true or no, which Paul himself teached, (Acts 17:11). For whosoever he be, yes, though he were an angel from heaven, if he teach matters contrary to the doctrine of the

Holy and Canonical Scriptures, we are to hold him accursed, yes, and accursed again, as the Apostle of Christ Jesus St. Paul commandeth, (Gal. 1:8, 9).

Again, the Church of Rome when it taught and holds that the Scriptures were to be read to the people or congregation in an unknown tongue, what were the people the wiser? St. Paul would have all things done to edifying in the Church: for St. Paul says, *Is qui supplet locum indocti, quomodo dicturus est Amen ad tuam gratiarum actionem, quando quidem quid dicas nescit?*—"How shall he that supplieth the place of an unlearned man say Amen to thy thanksgiving, seeing he understandeth not what thou sayest?" (1 Cor. 14:16). And in that whole chapter he utterly dislikes service in an unknown tongue. And therefore if the Church of Rome will not confess their error herein, she is past all shame, and has the impudent and shameless face of an harlot.

They have all devised and defended a place of purgatory, in which all that depart this life be put and there punished, (being a punishing fire) until they help to fetch them out with their masses and other their inventions and devices, which they will not do nor think they have reason to do, except they have good current coin for the same. And therefore it may be well and justly called *Purgatory pick–purse*; and it is manifestly apparent hereby, that wealth and great riches of the Clergy was the only mark they aimed at: for it has no warrant in the Canonical Books of the Scriptures; yes, the Canonical Books of Scriptures show the contrary, and so do the ancient

Fathers. Christ in the Gospel (Luke 16), shows only but two places, namely, heaven and hell; saying, that the rich man's soul (which was unmerciful to Lazarus) went after his death to hell, and there was tormented, and that Lazarus's soul (he being dead) was carried into Abraham's bosom, a place of joy and comfort. To the thief which was executed at the passion and suffering of Christ, and believed in Him, Christ answered, *Hodie eris mecum in Paradiso:*—"This day shalt thou be with Me in Paradise," (Luke 23:43); which shows that the souls of the faithful never come in Purgatory-fire to be boiled and punished; for all their sin is forgiven, and consequently the punishment incident to the same is forgiven also, and their souls pass from death to life, and into Paradise, a place of comfort, delectableness, and all sweetness, namely, heaven, where Christ is. "Verily, verily, I say unto you, (Christ says,) he that heareth My word, and believeth on Him that sent Me, hath eternal life, and shall not come into condemnation, but is passed from death unto life," (John 5:24); what is become then of this Purgatory? St. Paul says, "I desire to depart and to be with Christ," (Phil. 1:23); showing by this that presently after his dissolution he was to be with Christ in glory. "For we know (he says) that if this earthly house of this tabernacle were dissolved, we have a building not made with hands, eternal in the heavens," (2 Cor. 5:1). St. John in his Revelation says, "Blessed are the dead which die in the Lord from henceforth: they rest from their labours, and their works do follow them," (Rev. 14:13). If from the time of their death they have blessedness and rest, (as he shows,) then are they not in any Purgatory-fire to be scorched and molested. St. Peter tells the saints and children of God, and assures them of it, "That the end of their faith is the salvation of their souls," (1 Peter 1:9). If salvation of their souls begin at the end of their faith, which lasts to the end of their life, (and no longer, for then they have the fruition and possession of that which they believe and hope for,) then it is manifest there is no Purgatory. Ambrose says, *Qui hic non receperit remissionem peccatorum, illic non erit is in caelo: quia remissio peccatorum vita aeterna est:*—He that here in this life does not receive remission of sins, shall never come into the kingdom of heaven: for life eternal is remission of sins.[90] Cyprian says, *Quando istinc excessum fuerit, nullus jam locus paenitentice, nullus satisfactionis effectus: hic vita aut amittitur aut tenetur: hic saluti aeternae cultu Dei et fructu providetur.*[91] And again by and by, he says, *Tu sub ipso licet exitu et vitae temporalis occam pro delictis Deum roges, qui verus et unus est; venia datur confitenti, et credenti indulgentia salutaris, et ad immortalitatem sub ipsa morte transitur:*—That is, When men are once departed hence, there is then no more place of repentance, no effect of satisfaction: here life is either lost or kept: here provision is made for eternal salvation by the worship of God, and fruits. And therefore, (he says,) do thou call upon God, though it be at thy last gasp and departure of this thy temporal life, but call upon that God

---

[90] Ambr. De Bono Mortis, lib. ii.
[91] Cyprian. Contra Demet., tract, i.

Chapter 5: The False Religion of the Church of Rome

which is one and true: pardon is given thee if thou confess thy sins, and saving forgiveness if thou believe; and from death presently thou shalt pass to immortality. Hierome says, that the time of sowing their seed for Christians is this present life, and that as soon as this life is ended, they reap everlasting life.[92] Augustine says, *Primum fides Catholicorum Divina authoritate regnum esse credit caelorum: secundum gehennam, ubi omnis apostata, vel a Christi fide alienus, supplicia experitur; tertium penitus ignoramus, nec esse in scripturis sanctis reperimus.* The first place (he says) the faith of Catholics do (by Divine authority) believe to be the kingdom of heaven; the second, hell; a third place we are utterly ignorant of, neither can we find any such in the Holy Scriptures. And the same Augustine writes in another place, *They which believe a Purgatory-fire are much deceived, and that through a human conceit.*[93] How then can the Papists be the true Catholics, which believe not the faith of the Catholics, which Augustine affirms?

They also hold, that a man, since the fall of Adam, has free-will of himself and of his own power to come to God, and to do things acceptable and well-pleasing in His sight: whereas God says after that time, "The imagination of men's hearts is only evil continually," (Gen. 6:5): if they be only evil, then have they of themselves no affection to goodness acceptable to Him. And Christ says, "No man can come to Me, except the Father draw him," (John 6:44). If

---

[92] Hier. In Gal 6.
[93] Aug., Enchir. ad Laurent., cap. 67.

he must be drawn before he can come, he has no proclivity or willingness of himself to come; and therefore it is that the Prophet says, "Heal me, O Lord, and I shall be healed," (Jer. 17:14); showing, that he has no power in himself to be changed. And St. Paul shows, that till God give grace, "there is none righteous, no, not one!" (Rom. 3:10): for all the philosophical virtues and good deeds which men do before they have faith (which is the gift of God) are sin, and not acceptable to God: for the Apostle witnesseth, "Without faith it is impossible to please God," (Heb. 11:6); and that "whatsoever is not of faith is sin," (Rom. 14:23). Christ Himself again says, "Except men be ingrafted into Him, they can bring forth no fruit," (John 15:1, 2). Paul often teaches that we must be new men, and "put off the old man," (Eph. 4:22). And again, he bids us to be renewed in the spirit of our mind, (Eph. 4:23). And moreover he says, "that the natural man receives not the things of the Spirit, neither can he, because they are spiritually discerned," (1 Cor. 2:14). And again, "that it is God that worketh the will and the deed," (Phil. 2:13). And he plainly confesses of himself and of all others, that we are not sufficient of ourselves to think anything of ourselves; and that "all our sufficiency is of God," (2 Cor. 3:5); which premises do show, that our understanding is blind, and our will perverse in any Divine matter, or acceptable service to God, till God do enlighten the one, and draw and move the other to Himself. Thus has God ordered matters, to the end Himself might have all the glory ascribed to Him, as good reason He should. For what is man since his fall in Adam,

Chapter 5: The False Religion of the Church of Rome

but an abject and runaway from God, of himself seeking by-paths, and crooked outways, leading from God, and from His worship, except he be assisted from above? (which is signified by Adam's hiding himself from the presence of God after his fall). And therefore Augustine sais well and truly, *Hominem libero arbitrio male usum, et se et illud perdidisse:*—That man having ill-used his free-will that he had, has now both lost himself, and that.[94] And again, *Liberum arbitrium captivatum, ne quid possit ad justitiam;*—That free-will is taken captive, that it can do nothing towards righteousness. And again, *Hominis non libera sed a Deo liberata voluntas obsequitur:*—Not the free-will, but the freed will of man (which is *set free by God*) obeys and yields obeyance. And again, *Liberum non fore, quod Dei gratia non liberavit:*—That the will is *bound* and *not* free, till God deliver it and set it at liberty. Cyprian (which St. Augustine so often cites) says, *De nullo gloriandum, etc.:*—Man must glory of nothing, because nothing is ours: therefore every man annihilating his own power, must learn wholly to depend upon God. And Chrysostom says, that *omnis homo non modo naturaliter peccator, sed totus peccatum est:*—Every man is not only sinful naturally, but is altogether sin.[95] And therefore St. Paul shows, that till a man be regenerate or born anew, and until he be renewed in the spirit of his mind, he has in him nothing else, but

---

[94] Aug. ad Arst., Epist. 44; Enchir. ad Lau., cap. 30, et lib. iii., cap. 7; et ad Bonif., cap. 8, et 3, et alibi passim.
[95] De Praedest. Sanct., ad Bonif., lib. iv., in Gen. Hom. i.

concupiscentias erroris;—lusts and affections after error, (Eph. 4:22); saying likewise, that by "nature we are the children of wrath," (Eph. 2:3). Which also Christ Himself testifies to Nicodemus, saying, "That which is born of the flesh is flesh, and that which is born of the Spirit is spirit," (John 3:6,) and that "except a man be born again, he cannot see the kingdom of God," (John 3:3). And therefore St. Paul tells, that there must be a "new creature," (2 Cor. 5:17,) whosoever will be in Christ Jesus, and a renewing and *metamorphosis* of the mind (he uses the very word) before men can find out the good and acceptable will of God, and what pleases Him. (Rom. 12:2). I therefore conclude, that the Papists are far wide, and does not know the misery and thraldom of men, where into they are fallen by that great sin and disobedience of Adam, whilst they stand to defend free-will in natural men. Indeed it appears to be free and too free to evil, but it is so bound and fast tied from desire of any Divine duties, that God must first draw it out of that servitude in which it is, and set it at liberty and move it to come, before it will show any readiness that way. I trust therefore they see, that their Church not only may err, but errs most grossly in many points.

They hold that in the Sacrament of the Lord's Supper it is lawful to debar the people of the cup; and so they use: which is contrary to the institution of Christ, *Bibite ex hoc omnes*,—"Drink ye all of it," (Matt. 26:27). And as well and by as good authority may they take the bread from the people likewise. And it is contrary to the express doctrine of St. Paul, (who, as himself testifies, delivered the institution of Christ,) for he says, "Let a man examine himself,"—*Et sic edat, et bibat:*—"and so let him eat of this bread, and drink of this cup," (1 Cor. 11:28). So that he must drink as well as he must eat. And that the people should be partakers and receive in both kinds, was observed many hundred years in the Church after Christ; insomuch, as Pope Gelasius decreed, that all they should be excommunicate, which would receive but in one kind. But Rome that now is, is not Rome that then was: but with her Council of Constance, is not ashamed to go against all antiquity and all divinity.[96]

But they hold (which is a marvelous gross error also) Transubstantiation in the Sacrament, namely, that after the words of consecration, the bread and wine are changed into the very substance of the body and blood of Christ; and this they would seem to ground upon these words, *Hoc est corpus meum*:—"This is My body," (Matt. 26:26,) which they will have to be expounded literally. But why then do they not expound the other words of Christ literally also concerning the cup? for the text says, in the twenty-seventh and twenty-eighth verses, that He took the cup, *etc.*, and said, "This is My blood." I am sure they will not say, that the cup was the blood of Christ, (as the words be,) but they will grant a figure in those words, namely, *Continens pro contento*, that by the cup is meant the wine in it. If then they will admit a figure in this, why may there not be a figure in the other? namely, *signatim pro signo*;

---

[96] Cap., Comperimus de consecra., dist. 2.

that these words, "This is My body," should be understood thus, *The bread is a sign of My body* (which was broken for you). If we look into the old sacraments of the Jews, namely, circumcision, and the Paschal Lamb, we shall find the phrase of speech observed: for circumcision was called the Lord's Covenant, when indeed it was not the Covenant (as all men do know) but a sign and seal of the Covenant: for the Covenant was this to Abraham, *Ego Deus tuus, et seminis tui, etc.* —"I will be thy God, and the God of thy seed," *etc.* (Gen. 17; Rom. 4). So likewise the Paschal Lamb is called the Passover, when indeed it was but a sign of the Passover or passing over or through the Red Sea, (which was a mighty and most wonderful deliverance, Pharaoh and all his host being drowned in the sea, when they passed through as on dry land). Insomuch therefore as it is usual in Sacraments so to speak, it is not against reason, but stands with very good reason, to think, that Christ Jesus in instituting this Sacrament, which to the Christians is the same that the Paschal Lamb was to the Jews, did likewise call the bread His body, in such sort as the Paschal Lamb was the Passover: that is to say, figuratively; that as the Paschal Lamb was called the Passover, and yet was but a sign and remembrance of their Passover; so the bread was called His body, and yet it was but a sign and remembrance of His body. And that this is the right exposition, may appear by the words of Christ, where He says, "This do in remembrance of Me," (Luke 22:19). Tertullian likewise so expounds them; for he says, Christ said, *Hoc est corpus Meum, id est, figura corporis Mei:*—

Chapter 5: The False Religion of the Church of Rome

"This is My body," that is, a *figure* of My body.[97] Augustine likewise says, *Christi miranda patientia adhibuit Judam ad convivium, in quo corporis et sanguinis Sui figuram discipulis tradidit*:—The admirable patience of Christ admitted Judas to the banquet, in which He delivered to His disciples a figure of His body and blood.[98] And again he says, *Non dubitavit Dominus dicere, Hoc est corpus Meum, cum daret signum corporis Sui*:—The Lord doubted not to say, This is My body, when He gave but the sign of His body.[99] And this exposition must necessarily be true: for St. Paul says plainly and expressly, that the communicant eats bread, (1 Cor. 11:26, 28): *Ergo*, it remains bread, after the words of consecration: for if it were transubstantiate into the body of Christ, then there were no bread to eat, but the body of Christ is the thing that should be eaten. But none do eat the very body of Christ: for if every communicant did eat the very body of Christ naturally, carnally, and really, (as they grossly suppose,) Christ should have a number of bodies, which is palpably absurd and monstrous; and beside, then every communicant should be saved, yes, even Judas himself, (which is known to be the child of perdition,) for Christ says, "Whoso eateth My flesh, and drinketh My blood, has eternal life," (John 6:54). Indeed the elect and godly do eat Christ and drink Christ; but how? not carnally, but spiritually, and by a true faith, apprehending Christ, and applying Christ with all His

---

[97] Tertul. Cont. Marcion., lib. iv.
[98] Aug. in Psal. 8.
[99] August. in tom. vi., Cont. Adamant.

benefits as firmly to their souls, as the bread and wine is applied to their bodies. Besides, if Christ gave His body to be eaten really by His disciples, at the time of the institution of this Sacrament, what was it that did hang on the cross on the morrow? Moreover, St. Peter says, that as touching the body of Christ, the heavens must contain Him to the end of the world, (Acts 3:21). If His body be in heaven, and that He has a true body, (as all men know He has,) how can it be that He should be both in heaven and in earth, as touching His body, at one time? for though He have a glorified body, yet He retains the nature and property of a true body still; which can be but in one place at once. And so Augustine says, *Corpus Domini in quo resurrexit, uno tantum loco esse potest*:—The body of the Lord in which He rose again, can be but in one place only.[100] But the Papists, to help themselves, are driven to this, to say, that there is a miracle in the Sacrament, and that Christ is there miraculously. To this I answer, that if the bread be turned into the very body of Christ by a miracle, then should it appear visibly so; for the nature of every miracle is to be visible to the outward eye and senses; as when Christ turned water into wine, it was visibly wine; when Moses's rod was turned into a serpent, it was visibly a serpent: and so if the bread be turned into the very body of Christ, it is visibly His body, if you will hold a miracle to be wrought in it. But Augustine answereth, there is no miracle in the Sacrament, saying thus: *Honorem tanquam*

---

[100] Aug. in Job., Tract. 3.

Chapter 5: The False Religion of the Church of Rome

religiosa, possunt habere, stuporem tanquam mira non possunt:—The Sacraments may have honour as things religious, but they are not to be admired at as miracles.[101] Theodoret also is most express against Transubstantiation, for thus He says: *Neque enim signa mystica post sanctificationem recedunt a natura sua: manent enim in priore substantia, figura et forma, et videri et tangi postunt sicut prius:*—that is, The mystical signs after consecration do not depart from their nature; for they abide still in their former substance, figure, and form, and may be both seen and felt as before.[102] Gelasius, a Pope himself, says most plainly, that there is no Transubstantiation in the Sacrament: his words be these: *Non desinit substantia vel natura panis et vini; et certe imago et similitudo corporis et sanguinis Christi in actione myteriorum corporis Christi celebratur:*—The substance or nature of bread and wine Does not cease, and verily there is the image and similitude of the body and blood of Christ, celebrated in the action of the mysteries of the body of Christ.[103] And therefore I conclude that the Church of Rome which now is, is not the same which it was in former times, but it is become degenerate and revolted from that former purity, which once was in it; and consequently it is expressly manifest that that Church both may and do err.

The Church of Rome further holds, that their Pope has authority to depose kings and princes. But by what title? It is clear that in his either so doing, or attempting to

---

[101] Aug., tom. iii., De Trinit., lib. iii., cap. 10.
[102] Theod. Dialog. Ii.
[103] Gelas. Contra Eutych.

do, he is both a notable traitor to God, whose authority he claims and arrogates, and to princes, to whom he should be subject: for the raising and pulling down of princes God has reserved to Himself alone, in His power: for it is He (not the Pope) that deposes the mighty from their seats, and exalts them that are of low degree, (Luke 1:53); it is He (not the Pope) that puts down kings, and gives kingdoms to whomsoever He will, (Dan. 2:21); and it is He that testifies of Himself, saying, *Per Me reges regnant, et principes dominantur:*—"By Me kings reign and princes bear dominion," (Dan. 4:17). Seeing therefore it is God that has this high authority proper to Himself, which way can the Pope claim it, without injury and treason to God? Will he claim it by reason of his keys, and in his apostolical right? That he cannot do; for he must remember that the keys given were the keys of the kingdom of heaven, (Matt. 16:19); and therefore by authority of the keys he cannot meddle with terrestrial kingdoms, to open an entrance for any into them, or to shut out, or exclude, any that be in them. And beside St. Paul the Apostle says expressly both of himself and of the rest of the Apostles, that how great authority soever they have for the overthrowing of strongholds, (that is, of rebellious thoughts, and proud conceits, and stiffnecked opinions seated in men's hearts against God, as himself expounds in the same place,) that all their power and means to convert men is only by the sword of the Spirit, which is the Word of God, and by the power of the keys committed to them. In all which their authority, given to them from Christ, he confesses plainly, that the weapons of their warfare are not carnal, but mighty through God, that is, spiritual: (2 Cor. 10:4): which words do demonstrate, that by their ecclesiastical ministry they have clearly no civil authority committed to them. And moreover it is manifest, by the practice of the Apostles, and all their precepts, (commanding all Christians to obey their rulers, their kings, and princes, yes, though they were persecutors,) that the Apostles never had any such authority committed to them; (Rom. 13:1–4; 1 Peter 2:13; Titus 3:1); and therefore it is undoubtedly true, that the Pope of Rome cannot claim it by any such authority. Again, the Bishop of Rome can claim no more authority by the power of the keys, or of binding and loosing, than any other bishop elsewhere may do; for the keys, that is to say, the power of opening and shutting, and of binding and loosing, were given to all the rest of the Apostles as well as to Peter; (John 20:22, 23); and consequently for any minister of the Gospel thereby to claim authority above another, is absurd; for they be all indifferently joined in one commission, and therefore have all equal authority; and therefore the Bishop of Rome by virtue of the keys has no more authority than any other bishop has; that is to say, none at all to depose princes. Their duty is rather to practise obedience themselves to them, and to teach the same obedience to others as the Apostles of Christ did. Yes, Christ Himself said, "My kingdom is not of this world," (John 18:36). Himself likewise refused to be made a king, (John 6:15). Himself paid tribute to Caesar, and commanded others to give the same, and all other duties of subjection and obedience to Caesar, (Matt. 22:21). If He were subject to Caesar, it is a shame for the Bishop of Rome to exalt himself above Caesar.

But perchance the Bishop of Rome will challenge this his sovereign authority over princes by donation from Constantine or some other Christian Emperor. Indeed such fables sometimes he is not ashamed to utter: but let it be the strongest way for him, if you will, that some Christian Emperor was so foolish as to give him his empire, which is neither likely nor credible, yet say I, it was neither lawful, nor tolerable for him to take it, if he will be a minister of the Gospel, or successor of the Apostles: for Christ has expressly forbidden His Apostles, and in them all the ministers of the Gospel, all such dominion and civil jurisdiction, saying thus to them, *The princes of the Gentiles exercise dominion over them, and they that are great exercise authority upon them; but it shall not be so among you;* (Matt. 20:25,26; Mark 10:42, 43; Luke 22:25, 26); which words be most prohibitory, and show that they may not reign like kings of nations, nor bear rule as great men in those nations do; but they must serve in the Church, be diligent to discharge that great charge in the Church which their Master Christ Jesus has laid upon them. And therefore every way the Pope of Rome has no title, but is hereby an usurper, and an intruder, and a notorious and odious traitor, both to God and princes. And besides, all the ancient Churches have affirmed and acknowledged the supreme authority of princes, above and over all, both priests and people. And therefore Tertullian says, *Colimus*

Chapter 5: The False Religion of the Church of Rome

Imperatorem ut hominem a Deo secundum, et solo Deo minorem:—We honour the Emperor as the next man to God, and inferior to God only.[104] And again he says, that princes are *a Deo secundi, post Eum primi, ante omnes, et super omnes:*—The second to God, the first next after God, and before and over all men.[105] Optatus in like sort says, *Super Imperatorem non est nisi solus Deus, qui fecit Imperatorem:* —There is none above the Emperor, but God only which made the Emperor.[106] And Chrysostom says, *Parem vllum super terram non habet:*—He has no equal on earth.[107] And Gregory, Bishop of Rome, himself affirms, that the power is given to princes from heaven, not only over soldiers, but priests.[108] And therefore I conclude that the Church of Rome which now is, is not the Church which once it was, but is wonderfully fallen into corruption, and grown into pride, both against God, and His anointed prince; and consequently not only may err, but does err, and that most detestably, and abominably in the highest degree.

The Bishop of Rome further holds, that he has authority from God to forgive sins; and thereupon he sends from his charters of pardon, his bulls and indulgences, to such as he means to assault. The Scriptures in the Gospel could say, "Who can forgive sins but God only?" (Mark 2:7). If therefore the Pope of Rome will take upon him to

---

[104] Tertul. Ad Scap.
[105] Tertul. in Apologet.
[106] Optatus, Cont. Parmen., lib. xiii.
[107] Chrysost., Ad Populum Antioch., homil. ii.
[108] Gregor., Epist., lib. iii., cap. 100, 103.

forgive sins (in that sort he does) he must prove himself to be God; otherwise his actions will not be warranted. How often in the Scriptures it is said of God, that He forgives iniquity and transgressions ascribing that authority only to God, and to no other. I need not recite any particular places, the whole *Book* of God is plentiful herein. I do not deny but Ministers of the Gospel have power to bind and loose sinners; (as Christ Himself shows, Matt. 16:19); but how and whom? They can neither justify the unrighteous, whom God abhors, not yet condemn the godly and faithful, whom God dearly loveth. Inasmuch therefore as they cannot pardon such as God condemneth, nor yet condemn such whom God acquits, (Rom. 8:33, 34,) it is manifest that all their power of binding and loosing sinners is limited and bounded within the compass of God's Word, which they may not pass; for if they do, they go beyond their warrant, and so all that they do will be of no force. The incredulous and obstinately wicked persons, they may, by warrant of God's Word, pronounce condemnation against, except they do repent; and to the assuredly faithful, repentant, and godly persons, whose continual care is to please God, and walk in His ways, they may pronounce the sentence of undoubted and certain salvation, because the Word of God affirms as much; and this is all the binding and loosing of sinners which they have: for in all their pronunciations of pardons, and forgiveness of sins, they must be sure they do not speak in their own names, nor their own wills and pleasures, but they must do it in the name of God, being first assured that it is His Word, will, and pleasure, which they utter. But the Bishop of Rome does not observe the rule of God's Word to square and measure his pardon by, but pardons whom he wishes, and as he wishes, as if he were a god himself, having absolute power in himself (without respect of God's word or will) to do what he wishes. Insomuch as traitors and rebels against God and their lawful princes, he will not only pardon without exception, but he will abet them in their damnable courses, till at last (when it is too late for them to repent) they will (if they take not good heed in time) feel the smart of it in *hell-torments* together forever. What the religion of Rome is, may appear by this, that any man for money may get a pardon for his sins; and then what sin need rich men fear to commit, when a Pope's pardon will salve all? or how can it be otherwise than a religion of licentiousness, when for money a man may have a license or dispensation against any sin whatsoever? These things be such open blots to the Romish religion, as that worthily every good or godly mind has it in detestation, and does justly condemn it. Yet further will I prove, that the Church of Rome cannot be the true Church possibly.

1. The Church of Rome holds, that the Divine and Sacred Scriptures do not contain all things necessary to salvation: but their unwritten traditions must (forsooth) all be received with equal and like authority: for so has their Council of Trent determined; and Pope Leo the Fourth does not fear to pronounce with a loud voice, That he that does not receive without difference the Popish

Canons, as well as the four Gospels, does not believe aright, nor hold the Catholic faith effectually.[109] The Decretal Epistles also they number with the Canonical Scriptures. And Pope Agatho says, that all the sanctions and decrees of their Romish See are to be taken as established by the Divine voice: which blasphemies who can abide? for hereby they make both the Scriptures imperfect; and not so content, do further add to those Scriptures. In which they commit two notable sins: first, accusing the Sacred and Canonical Scriptures, that they contain not all matters necessary to salvation: which is directly contrary to the testimony of St. John, who says, "These things are written that ye may believe, and that in believing you may have, life eternal;" and clean contrary to the testimony of St. Paul, who says, The Scriptures (given by Divine Inspiration) "are profitable to reprove, to teach, to correct, to instruct, and perfect the man of God," (2 Tim. 3:15); *Ergo*, the Scriptures, or Word of God written, is a true, sound, and perfect whole doctrine, containing in itself fully all things needful for our salvation. Yes, St. Paul says expressly to Timothy, "The Scriptures are able to make him wise unto salvation," (2 Tim. 3:15). And therefore the Church of Rome being clean contradictory, marvelously errs; and therefore also we need none of their unwritten traditions. And again, how should we be assured that those traditions which they call apostolical, be apostolical, considering them not written by the

---

[109] Concil. Trident., decret. i., sess. iv., distinct. 20, cap. In libellis; dist. 15, cap. In Canon.; dist. 15, cap. Sic omnes.

Chapter 5: The False Religion of the Church of Rome

Apostles? Augustine speaking of this says thus, *Si quae reticuit Jesus Christus, quis nostrum dicet hocvel illud esse?—Et si quis hoc dicat, quomodo probabit?*—That is, If Jesus Christ have kept anything close, which of us shall say it is this or that? And if any say, it is this, how will he prove it?[110] for all the errors of the Church of Rome shroud themselves under the harbour of traditions. And Chrysostom says flatly, Whatsoever is requisite for our salvation, is contained in the Scriptures.[111] And again he says, All things be clear and manifest in the Scriptures, and whatsoever things be needful be manifest there.[112] And Hierome in the Prologue of the Bible to Pauline, after he had recited the Books of the New Testament and the Old, says in this way: I pray thee (dear brother) among these live, muse upon these, does not know otherwise, seeks for none other thing. And again, upon the Books of the Old and New Testament: These Writings are holy, these Books are sound, there is none other to be compared to these; whatsoever is beside these, may in no wise be received amongst these holy things. And again he says, All other things which they seek out or invent at their pleasure, without the authority and testimony of the Scriptures (as though they were the traditions of the Apostles) the Word of God cuts off.[113] Let us therefore stand fast to the written Word of God; and as for their traditions, which they cannot prove, but obtrude

---

[110] August, in Epist. ad Januar.
[111] Chrysost. in Mat. 24, hom. iv.
[112] Chrysost. in 2 Thess. 2.
[113] Hierome upon Haggai 2.

to us without testimony of Scriptures, let us contemn them. For as Athanasius says, The Holy Scriptures inspired from God are sufficient to all instruction of the truth.[114] And as for the other point of the Papists in equalling and adding their traditions, their decretal epistles and canons, to the pure and Divine Word of God, it is blasphemy intolerable, and who can endure it? For Does not God say thus: "Ye shall not add unto the word which I command you, neither shall ye diminish aught from it," (Deut. 4:2). And again He says: "What thing soever I command you, observe to do it; thou shalt not add thereto, nor diminish from it," (Deut. 12:32). And does not St. John in his Revelation say, "If any man shall add unto these things, God shall add unto him the plagues which are written in this Book, and shall take away his part out the Book of Life?" (Rev 22:18, 19). I conclude therefore, that the Church of Rome, which Does not content herself with the Sacred Scripture, (which the chaste spouse of Christ evermore does,) is not the true Church of God: for there she shows herself to bear the mark of a strumpet. But when she proceeds and adds her own traditions, decretal epistles, and canons, to the Word written; and makes them to be of as good and equal authority as the Canonical and Sacred Scriptures themselves; what greater pride could have been shown, or what higher blasphemy? But these are the right notes of an adulteress to equal herself with her husband. Yes, what should I say more? They hold, that the authority of the Church is above the Scriptures, which shows fully

---

[114] Athanas. Contra Geut.

Chapter 5: The False Religion of the Church of Rome

the notable pride and spiritual whoredom of their Church.

2. The Church of Rome is idolatrous, and therefore it is not the true Church. They fall down before idols and images, as the heathen did, and therefore commit idolatry as the heathen did; I speak of the manner of their worship; for the heathen, howsoever they worshipped not the true God, yet they thought they worshipped the true God, and their meaning was to worship the true God in the image or idol, as the Papists likewise do mean; for they say they be not such fools as to think, or believe, that an image or idol (made of wood or stone) could be God; neither were the heathen so foolish as to think or believe that their idols or images were God, (for they knew they were made of wood or stone, or such like); but (as they took it) they worshipped God in the image, as the Papists say they do; and therefore the case for the manner of worship is all one. Again, if the Papists do not worship the idol or image, why do they bow down to it? God commands, saying, "Thou shalt not make unto thee any graven image," (Exod. 20:4); so that the very making of images to represent God with it (who is a Spirit eternal and invisible) is idolatry. Again he says, "Thou shalt not how down thyself to them, nor serve them," *etc.* (Exod. 20:5). So that to bow down to them (though they be supposed to represent God) is idolatry; for God must be worshipped in such sort as Himself has prescribed, and not otherwise. And that it is flat idolatry to worship God in any image, is expressed and manifest by the children of Israel, when they made the golden calf to be a representation of God; for the text shows that it was

idolatry, for which many of them were plagued and punished, (Exod. 32); and yet their meaning was to worship the true God in the calf: for they were not so simple as to think, or believe, that that dead idol or image was God, and therefore the idolatry of the Church of Rome is as gross and wicked as theirs was. Neither can the Papists help themselves in their accustomed distinction of δουλεία, and λατρεία, affirming that they give to images but *duliam* that is, service; and to God *latriam*, that is, worship; showing thereby, that both they worship God, and serve images. "But how agreeth the temple of God with images?" Paul says; (2 Cor. 6:16); or what warrant have they to serve images beside God, when Christ Himself says, (It is written) "Thou shalt worship the Lord thy God, and Him only shalt thou serve?" (Matt. 4:10). And Paul the Apostle likewise persuades expressly, that men should turn from idols, (or images, to serve the living and true God, (where the word *Dulia* is used,) by which the Apostle shows, that there is such an opposition between images and the service of God, that he that serves the one cannot serve the other, (1 Thes. 1:9). God Himself dislikes idols and images utterly, saying by the Prophet Habakkuk that they are so far from being laymen's books (as the Papists term them) that they are no better than teachers of lies. And John himself commands all Christians to keep themselves from idols, (1 John 5:21). Besides, it is idolatry to pray to any but God; for Christ bids, when men pray, not to call upon the Virgin Mary, nor any other saint departed this life, but on God alone. "After this manner (he says) pray ye, Our Father which art in heaven," *etc.* (Matt. 6:9). Again, St. Paul says, "How shall they call on Him in whom they have not believed?" (Rom. 10:14); declaring thereby, that faith and prayer go together. We can call upon none, but we must consequently also believe on him: but we are to believe on none but God; therefore we may pray to none but God; and therefore the Church of Rome calling upon saints departed, commits gross idolatry; for the Scripture shows, that God only is to be prayed to. Besides, they teach in their idolatrous mass, or sacrament of the altar (as they term it) after a certain mumbling of words by the priest, there is no bread nor wine remaining, but the very body and blood of Christ; and that piece of bread which is shown (for bread it still appears to be, for all their magical mumbling) they command to be adored and worshipped. To adore or worship any creature (such as bread is) is idolatry. The Papistical Church does the same: *ergo*, it is idolatrous. I have proved it before, that it remains bread after the consecration; and that Christ cannot possibly be there, as touching the bodily substance, because in that respect He is ascended up into heaven, and there sits on the right hand of God His Father, until He come to judge the quick and the dead. And if they will not believe Divine testimonies in it, yet the authority of Cicero, a heathen man, might somewhat move them; for in one place he says, *Quem tam amentem esse putas, qui ilium quo vescatur, Deum credat esse?* that is, Whom do you think so mad, as to believe that which he eats to be God?[115] Insomuch therefore as the Church of Rome worships bread as if it were God, it is manifest, they be gross idolaters; and consequently their Church cannot be the true Church of God on earth.

    3. The Papists do not deny Christ in words, but if we examine them by particulars, we shall find that in deed they do. As for example, we know that the right faith believes Christ Jesus to be both God and man, which the Church of Rome in words will also affirm: but urge them in this point of the Sacrament, and then they bewray themselves, that they believe not Christ to have a true body; for when they are pressed with this, that the body of Christ cannot be both in heaven and in earth at one and the self-same time, because it is against the nature of a true body so to be; then they become *Ubiquitaries*, and say that because the Godhead of Christ is everywhere, therefore His humanity is everywhere. But this is no good consequent; for the Godhead and humanity are of several natures. And if His body and flesh were everywhere, as His Godhead is, how is that true which the angel spoke, saying, *Surrexit, non est hic*:—"He is risen, He is not here?" (Matt. 28:6); for these words show that His body and flesh is not everywhere. Again, if He were everywhere in respect of His humanity, how is it true that He ascended into heaven? For that word,—*ascension*, shows that His bodily presence did remove from one place to another; and then was it not in

---

[115] Cicero De Natura.

that place from where it did remove. Lastly, It is the property of a Divine nature to be everywhere, and therefore whilst they defend this ubiquity of the flesh of Christ, it is as much as if they should say, that the flesh of Christ is turned into God, (which is a gross heresy). And thus it appears, that the Papists do, with the Eutychians, deny that Christ has a true body, when they hold that (contrary to the nature of a true body) it may be in divers places at once, yes, everywhere; and therefore denying Christ to have a true body, they are not the true Church. And so much for their error concerning the Person of Christ.

  4. Now for the office of Christ (for His Person and His office be two chief things which we are all to regard). The Papists will yield with us, that it consists in these three points, namely, that He is both a Prophet, a Priest, *and* a King. This, I say, in words they will acknowledge, but in deeds and verity they do not: for in respect that Christ is our Prophet, which should and did reveal His Father's will to the world, we ought to be content with His voice, and search no further than He has revealed in the Scriptures. But the Papists are not so contented, but they hold that their unwritten traditions, and Popish canons, must also be received upon like peril of damnation, as before I shown. Concerning the priesthood of Christ, it consists in two things, namely, the offering up of Himself once for a full, perfect, and sufficient sacrifice, and His intercession with His Father, which yet remains also, and shall do to the world's end. Both these the Papists annihilate, as I will prove. First, concerning the sacrifice

and oblation of Christ, there is no doubt, but being once done upon the cross, it was a most full, perfect and satisfactory sacrifice, to deliver both a *culpa et paena*, from the guiltiness, and the punishment incident to that guiltiness; for otherwise, how should Christ be Jesus, that is, a Saviour, if He did not deliver us from the punishment, as well as from the sin? (Matt. 1:21). But the Papists hold that Christ has obtained by His passion remission for our sins going before baptism; but for sins committed after baptism, that His passion has taken away only the guiltiness, that the punishment remains notwithstanding; which is to be paid in purgatory (as they say) and to be redeemed by our own satisfactions; and so they make the punishment due to sin (which is indeed eternal in hell) to be but temporary in Purgatory, upon satisfactions (as they have devised). But what can a man give for the ransom of his soul? And it appears before, even by the report of Augustine, that the Catholic faith believes no Purgatory, such as they have invented: for as St. John says, "The blood of Jesus Christ cleanseth us from all sin," (1 John 1:7): and that His most precious blood is the only Purgatory we hold, and delivers His people from the punishment due to sins, as well as from sins; for our punishment was laid upon Him, and with His stripes we are healed, as the Prophet Isaiah speaks, (Isa. 53). Again, the Papists do say, they offer up Christ in their mass, which mass they say is propitiatory, both for the living and the dead. First, for the dead it cannot be propitiatory, nor do good to; for as the tree falls, so it lies, and as a man is found to die, so he go either to heaven or to hell. A third place which the Papists call *Purgatory*, there is not. And if any be in heaven, their masses can do them no good; for they enjoy all good already. And if any man be in hell, we know that *Ex inferno nulla redemptio*:—From hell there is no redemption. And therefore for the dead it cannot be propitiatory, nor any thing else available; and for the living it cannot be propitiatory. Yes, it is blasphemous and derogatory to the passion of Christ once for all; for inasmuch as "He is a Priest for ever, after the order of Melchisedec," (Heb. 5:6). He is to die but once, which He did upon the cross; whose oblation being perfect (as the author to the Hebrews speaks) needed not any other help (as of mass, or whatsoever else) to make it perfect yes, it is wicked, gross, blasphemous, and damnable to suppose any imperfection in the sacrifice and oblation of Jesus Christ: for God twice cried with a loud voice from heaven, saying, "This is My beloved Son, in whom I am well pleased," (Matt. 3:17; 17:5).

  5. As touching the other part of His Priesthood, namely, His intercession with His Father, by which He makes request to God for us, although the Papists ascribe that chiefly to Christ; yet what do they else but clean rob Him of it, when they associate others with Him? And namely the Virgin Mary, they call her the Queen of Heaven, the Gate of Paradise, their life and sweetness, the Treasure of Grace, the Refuge of Sinners, and the Mediatrix of Men. I pray, what do they now leave to Christ? Yes, when they say thus to her, *O felix puerpera nostra pians scelera, jure matris impera Redemptori*:—That is, O happy Mother satisfying for

our sins, by thy motherly authority command the Redeemer. What greater blasphemy to Christ could they have uttered? It is clear that St. Paul says, "There is one God, and one Mediator between God and men, the Man Christ Jesus," (1 Tim. 2:5). But the Papists be not content with Him, but will have many mediators. St. Paul says moreover, "that by Him we have boldness and access unto God," (Eph. 3:12); and therefore what foolish fear is it of Papists to appoint to themselves other mediators? Since therefore the Church of Rome Does not repute the one oblation of Jesus Christ, and His intercession to be perfect, but accuses them of imperfection (as appears by their doctrine), it cannot possibly be the true Church. Christ Himself bids to ask in no other name than His, and promises that whatsoever shall be asked in His name it shall be done, (John 14:13,14). Chrysostom, speaking of the woman of Canaan, who, though she were a sinner, was bold to come to Christ, says thus: *En prudentiam hujus mulieris; non precatur Jaccbum, non supplicat Johanni, non adit ad Petrum, nec Apostolorum caetum respicit, aut ullum eorum requirit: sed pro his omnibus paenitentiam sibi comitem adjungit. et ad ipsum fontem progreditur:*—Behold the wisdom of this woman: she Does not pray James, she Does not beseech John, she does not go to Peter, she does not look to the company of the Apostles, neither requests of any of them; but for all this she takes repentance for her companion, and goes to the very fountain itself.[116] And again he says that to have access

---

[116] Chrysot. Hom. xii. de Cananaea.

to God, *Nihil opus est atriensi servo vel intercessore, sed dic, miserere mei Deus: is enim te audit quocunque sis loco, et undecunque invocetur;*—We have no need of any courtly attendant or intercessor, but say, Have mercy upon me, O God: for He hears you in what place soever you are; and from what place soever you call upon Him. Ambrose likewise answers the carnal reason of the Papists: *Solent* (he says) *misera uti excusalione, dicentes, per istos posse ire ad Deum, sicut per comites itur ad reges. Ideo ad regem per tribunos et comites itur, quia homo utique est rex: ad Deum autem, quem ut que nihil latet, suffragatore non est opus, sed mente devota. Ubieunque enim talis locutus fuerit, respondebit illi:*—that is, they are accustomed to use a pitiful excuse, saying, By these (saints) they may have access to God, as by earls there is access to kings. Therefore is it that by officers and earls access is made to the king, because the king himself is a man. But to come to God (from whom nothing is hid) there is no need of a spokesman, but of a devout mind; for wheresoever such a one speaks to Him, He will answer him.[117] The Church of Rome therefore, which does not account of the sufficiency and perfection of that one oblation of Christ, nor of His continual intercession, cannot possibly be the true Church.

  6. The Papists in words will not deny but Christ is a King which has all power in heaven and in earth: but indeed it appears they do exile and banish Him out of His kingdom, or at least leave Him but a small portion, or rather none at all; for in respect that He is a spiritual King,

---

[117] Amb. In Rom.

and the King of His Church, He is also (as St. James speaks) the only Lawgiver to this, and therefore by His laws only the Church is to be governed, which they cannot abide: for they add their Popish canons, constitutions, and customs, by which they will have the Church governed: yes, they will have these take place, though they utterly displace the Word of God, for their maintenance.

Secondly, Christ only is to reign in the consciences of men, and yet the Pope claims power to bind men's consciences by his laws, statutes, and decrees. Thirdly, he claims most traitorously to be the head of the whole universal Church, which title by way of prerogative is given and attributed only to Jesus Christ (to whom it only appertained). But before I proceed any further herein, I demand of the Pope and Papists, when, and by what right, he their proud Pope takes on him this title to be head of the Church, or universal Bishop over all the Christian world, (by virtue of which title he takes on him to rule as he wishes, and to do what he wishes). First, to claim it as successor to Peter, is impossible; for that Peter the Apostle never had any such title, preeminence, or authority over the rest of the Apostles. It is true, that Christ said to Peter, (after he had confessed Christ to be that Christ, the Son of the living God,) "Thou art Peter, and upon this rock will I build My Church," (Matt. 16:18). These words hitherto give no superiority to Peter, above the rest, only they show that the Church is built *non super Petrum, sed super Petram:—* not upon the person of Peter but upon the rock: and upon what rock? namely, upon that Christ Jesus whom Peter confesses to be the Son of the living God; for that confession of Peter concerning Jesus to be that Christ the Son of the living God, is the rock whereupon the Church is builded; for as St. Paul expounds and affirms, "Other foundation can no man lay than that which is laid, which is Jesus Christ," (1 Cor. 3:11). And in another place he says expressly, that "that Rock was Christ," (1 Cor. 10:4). And Christ Himself affirms likewise, "Whosoever heareth My words, and doeth them, I will liken him, unto a wise man which built his house upon a rock," (Matt. 7:24); showing thereby that He, and His words and doctrine, be the Rock, against which the gates of hell shall never prevail. Agreeable to this speaks St. Paul again when he says, that the Church is built "upon the foundation of the Apostles and Prophets, Jesus Christ Himself being the chief cornerstone," (Ephes. 2:20). Where then shall we find that Peter was made prince of the Apostles, to rule over all the rest, as the Pope now does? The Papists answer, that in the next words, when Christ gave to Peter by special name the keys of binding and loosing, he thereby made Peter the prince and universal bishop of the whole Church, (Matt. 16:19). But to this I say, that Christ in it gave no authority more to Peter than to the rest; that at this time the keys were not given to him, nor to the rest, only there was a promise that they should be given for the words be not in the present tense, *Do tibi*; I give unto thee; but in the future sense, *Dalo tili*,— I will give unto thee: which promise of Christ was afterward truly performed, (John 20:22, 23,) and when it was performed, the keys, that is, the power of binding and loosing sinners, was given not only to Peter, but to Peter and all the rest together, as St. John in his Gospel clearly declares and promises. Now because Peter was the man that gave answer for himself and the rest, therefore our Savior Christ spoke personally to Peter; and so both Cyprian and Augustine do expound and declare it. Otherwise, neither in the promise of the keys, nor yet in the receipt of the same, did Peter receive any more authority or superiority than the rest of the Apostles did. I grant he was called *primus*, because he was of the first that was called to the Apostleship; or because he was the first of all the Apostles that confessed Christ to be the Messiah and Son of the living God; or because he was readiest always to speak and answer. But all this Does not prove that he had authority over the rest, or a larger commission than the rest. Yes, the words of their commissions do show the contrary, namely, that they had all equal authority; for it was in this way made to them all indifferently, and without putting a difference, namely, "Go ye therefore and teach all nations, baptizing them in the name of the Father, and of the Son, and of the Holy Ghost; teaching them to observe all things whatsoever I have commanded," (Matt. 28:19, 20). But over all that remains written, and you shall find that Peter was one of the twelve, equal with the rest, and their fellow, but not their lord. Where was Peter's superiority when Paul reproved him to his face? (Gal. 2:11); when being accused, he pleaded no privilege, but for the clearing of himself, and satisfaction of others, he answers to that accusation. Where was Peter's authority over the rest, when the rest sent him and John to Samaria? (Acts 8:14). In that he went at their sending, he plainly shows that he had no principality over them. Where was his preeminence, or authority, when in a Council held at Jerusalem, where the Apostles were, yet not Peter but James ruled the action, and according to his sentence was the decree made? (Acts 15:13, *etc.*). Yes, I say moreover, that when there was contention amongst the Apostles, who should be chief amongst them, Christ told them plainly, "The kings of the Gentiles exercise lordship over them; and they that exercise authority over them are called benefactors: but ye shall not be so; but he that is greatest among you, let him be as the younger; and he that is chief as he that doth serve," (Luke 22:25, 20). If the greatest must be as the least, what authority has he above the least? for then has the least as great authority as the greatest; that is, they have all equal authority. I marvel therefore what the Pope and Papists mean, contrary to the tenor of the commission of Christ, contrary to the practice of Peter himself, and contrary to this decree made by Christ of their equality, to say notwithstanding that Peter was prince of the Apostles, and had authority over them all; when, as indeed it is manifest by all the Scriptures, and course of his life, he neither claimed nor had any authority over the rest more than the rest had over him, and consequently the Pope of Rome can never claim that as successor to Peter, which was never in Peter his supposed predecessor. The Papists perceiving that the Scriptures make nothing for but against them, (because they would have the matter colored with some antiquity, or show of antiquity at the least,) have devised some counterfeit and forged authors (as Anacletus and Anicetus, and such like) to speak something for them. But the falsehood of all those, is discovered by other writers (if they be well marked). In Cyprian's time it was deemed a matter odious for any to take upon him to be bishop of bishops, as appears by that voice which he cries in the Council of Carthage. It was likewise decreed in the African Council, that none should be called priest, or priests, or arch-priest, or any such like. The Council of Nice did decree, that the Bishop of Rome should keep himself within the compass of his province, and not exceed his bounds; as likewise the Bishops of Antioch, Jerusalem, and Constantinople were to do the like. Other Councils did affirm as much (which, because they are sufficiently known, I need not to recite). But they all show, that at those times the Bishop of Rome had no greater jurisdiction than within his own province, and that he could not meddle within the provinces of other Bishops. And Hierome of his time says, that the Bishop of Eugubium, or any other the least see, is equal to the Bishop of Rome.[118] The title of universal bishop was much desired of John, Bishop of Constantinople, and much contention there was about it; but it was never obtained of the Bishop of Rome, until the time of Boniface the Third, who procured that title of Phocas, that wicked emperor of Rome: after which, the Bishops of Rome never ceased still to augment their dignity, and increase the pride of the

---

[118] Hier. ad Evagrium.

Romish See. And even at the very first time, when John, Bishop of Constantinople, sought to get that title of universal bishop to his see, Gregory, then Bishop of Rome, did himself stand against it mightily, and affirms that he could be no less than Antichrist whosoever did take to him that title. First therefore it is manifest, that until the time of Gregory, Bishop of Rome, a universal Bishop was not heard of in the Church, and Boniface the Third was the first Bishop of Rome that got this title, which was about six hundred years after Christ. And besides, how will the Bishop of Rome that now is, avoid himself to be Antichrist, since by the express determination of Gregory, Bishop of Rome, his predecessor, he is condemned for Antichrist, inasmuch as he has this title, and is not ashamed of it?[119] For what is this else, but to come in the place of Christ, and consequently to be Antichrist, usurping the prerogative title of Christ Jesus? But the Pope says, that though he claim thus to be the head of the Church, yet he Does not name himself to be otherwise than a ministerial head, and to be Christ's Vicar on earth. But why will he be so arrogant as to challenge this title, without lawful conveyance made to him from Christ, which he cannot show? For who dare take upon him to be a lieutenant to an earthly prince without letters patent first had from the prince? Again, the Church of Christ on earth being as a chaste spouse of her Husband and Head, Christ Jesus, neither can nor ought to acknowledge any other for her

---

[119] Vide Greg., lib. iv., Epist. 32, 34, 36, 38, 39; et lib. vi., Epist. 20, 28, 29, 30.

head than that her Husband to whom she had plighted her troth. Lastly, there can be no successor, but when the predecessor is gone and absent: but Christ is always present with His Church, according to His own words, "Lo, I am with you alway, even unto the end of the world," (Matt. 28:20); and therefore He can have neither successors nor vicar to represent His person, or to guide His Church: for His Spirit (since His bodily ascension) is the Guide and Governor of the Church in His room; (John 14:15, 16); for no man mortal is appointed to it. I conclude therefore, that for all these causes the Church of Rome cannot possibly be the true Church.

7. The Church of Rome Does not ascribe justification to faith in Christ Jesus only, but says that men's works be meritorious, and to them partly is justification to be ascribed: and so they make men's imperfect works to be causes of salvation, which is a gross error, even in the foundation or fundamental point. St. Paul says, "All are justified freely by His grace," (Rom. 3:24). If they be justified *gratis*, freely, (as he affirms,) then are they justified without any desert of theirs. And St. Paul sets down this axiom, "Therefore we conclude that a man is justified by faith without the deeds of the law," (Rom. 3:28). And the Apostle in very many places (of which mention shall be made hereafter) expressly excludes works from being any causes of our justification; for indeed they are the effects of it. And therefore it appears to be a true position, that faith only justifies, inasmuch as justification is (in the sight of God) imputed to our faith,

not to our works: "for Abraham believed God, and it was counted unto him for righteousness," as Paul speaks; (Rom. 4:3); and he shows that Abraham was not justified by works before God; for if Abraham were justified by works, he has whereof to glory; but not before God; and because he had not whereof to glory before God, therefore he was not justified in the sight of God. I grant that St. James in his second chapter says, that Abraham was justified by his works, when he offered up his son Isaac at God's commandment; and likewise that he says, "that a man is justified by works, and not by faith only." But before whom is he justified by works? Not before God, but before men, that is to say, his works do declare to men that faith by which he is justified before God. And that this is the meaning of St. James, may appear by that his saying, where he says, "Shew unto me thy faith by thy works; thou sayest thou hast faith," that is not enough, thy words do not prove it, thy works will; therefore (he says) show me *thy faith by thy works*. This word (*show me*) manifests what manner of justification he speaks of, namely, that he speaks of a justification *before men*: for it is God that respects the faith of a man, by which only he is justified in His sight; and it is men which respect the works, by which indeed they testify to the world their faith to be good before God. For (as St. James says truly) "faith without works is dead," and not good, nor sound, nor available. But faith and works must go together: and indeed where a true faith is, there good works will show themselves as the fruits of it. And thus Paul and James are to be reconciled; which thing Thomas

Aquinas, a schoolman of the Papists, himself plainly testifies, saying, that Christ Jesus does justify effective—*effectually*; faith justifies apprehensive, by taking hold of Christ; and good works do justify declarative, that is, do declare to men their justification before God. And so it is clear, that howsoever a true faith cannot be without works, as fire cannot be without light and heat; yet our justification before God is to be imputed to our faith, not to our works; as warmth is to be imputed to the heat of the fire, not to the light of the fire: for so St. Paul says expressly, God imputes righteousness without works, (Rom. 4:6): and again, it is by grace, not of works, (Rom. 11:6); and again, not of works, (Rom. 9:11). Again, St. Paul tells the saints at Ephesus, that God has ordained men to walk in good works; yet he says that they may not trust to be saved by them; for he affirms and assures them, that they are saved by grace, and not of works, (Eph. 2:8, 9). Again, he speaks in the person of himself, and of all the children of God, and says, that we are saved not by works, but by His predestination and grace, (2 Tim. 1:9): and again, God is our Saviour, not for any works which we have done, but according to His mercy He has saved us, (Tit., 3:5): and divers other like places be. Wherefore Hilary has these very words (which we hold) *Sola fides justificat*:—Faith only justifies.[120] And Ambrose, among othe sentences, has this, *Non justificari hominem apud Deum nisi per fidem*:—That a man is not justified before God, but by faith:[121] which is as much

---

[120] Hila. in Mat. 8.
[121] Ambr. In Rom 3.

as faith only justifies before God. Basil says, That this is perfect and sound rejoicing in God, when a man Does not boast of his own righteousness, but knows that he lacks in himself true righteousness, and that he is justified by faith only: and Gregory Nazianzen says, That to believe only is righteousness. And therefore it is evident both by the express testimony of the Scriptures, and of the Fathers, that we hold the truth in this behalf, and that the Church of Rome is in a marvelous error. It is true which is written, that every man shall be rewarded according to his works; because the faith of men is esteemed and estimated by their works, as the tree is known by the fruit. But there is no text of Scripture to show, that any man is saved *propter merita*,— for his works or merits; but many texts of Scripture to the contrary, as before appears: for when we have done all that we can, yet we must say, (as Christ commandeth,) "We are unprofitable servants," (Luke 17:10); and therefore the Papists, which teach works meritorious, yes, works of supererogation available to salvation, as well for others as for themselves, hold not the right faith, and consequently are not the true Church.

But if I should show all the corruptions of the Romish Church, I should be infinite, neither am I able to number them. I will therefore conclude all this discourse only with this argument following: The Pope of Rome being the head of that Church, is that famous Antichrist that was foretold by Paul the Apostle, and that is prefigured in the Revelation of St. John: *ergo*, it is impossible that the Church of Rome should be the true

Church; for the Church of Antichrist (though it boast never so much) cannot be the true Church, though it would fain be so accounted; as many an harlot desires to be reputed an honest woman.

    1. One mark of that Antichrist, Paul shows to be this, He should exalt himself above all that is called God, (2 Thes. 2:4); he Does not say above God, but above all that is called God. Now those whom the Scripture calls *gods*, we know to be such as be the judges and magistrates of the earth, (Psa. 82:6,) who for that they be in the place of God, and His lieutenants, are vouchsafed (in Scripture) this high and honorable title of gods. That the Pope of Rome is such a one as exalts himself above any such god of the earth, namely, above all princes and magistrates, is a thing so well known, as I need not to prove it; himself by his wicked practices, and his Jesuits, seminaries, and priests, do in their books manifest the same to the world.

    2. Another mark of Antichrist St. Paul sets down to be this, namely, "He as God should sit in the temple of God, shewing Himself that He is God," (2 Thes. 2:4). And I pray, what does the Pope else do, but sit in the temple of God *as God?* who claiming the Apostolic See, he takes on him to be the head of the Church, and to rule as he wishes; to erect princes, and to depose them again from their thrones; that he cannot err, that he can forgive sins, matters that belong particularly to God, and to no other. What does he else do but by these demonstrations show himself to be God, insomuch as he arrogates to himself most proudly the authority of God Himself? which things the sixth book of

the Decretals, the Clementines, and the Extravagants do abundantly testify. For these men were not content with that which Angelicus wrote in his poetry, the beginning whereof is, *Papa stupor mundi:*—the Pope is the wonder of the world: *Nec Deus es, nec homo, sed Neuter, et inter utrumque:*—Thou art not God, neither art thou man; but Neuter, mixed of both. But these Popes were bold to take to themselves the very name of God, and to accept it, given of others; according as Pope Sixtus the Fourth, when he should first enter into Rome in his dignity Papal, had made for him a pageant of triumph, cunningly fixed upon that gate of the city he should enter in at, having written upon it this blasphemous verse, dedicated to him:

Oraculo vocis mundi moderaris habenas,
Et merito in terris crederis esse Deus.

By oracle of thine own voice the world thou governest all,
And worthily *a god* on earth men think, and do thee call.

Yes, shall I say more? The Pope (if any man in the world) takes upon him much more than *Luciferian pride,* howsoever to deceive the world with words) he calls himself *servus servorum Dei,*—a servant of the servants of God, that he exalts himself above God Himself, and His worship; for he takes upon him to be above the Scriptures, and to dispense with them at his pleasure, and to allow matters contrary to them; which God Himself (whose will is immutable, and revealed in it) will not do, for He and His Word will not be contrary. Again, by this it is manifest, that he exalts himself above God, inasmuch as there is less danger and punishment, for any that breaks any of God's laws, than for one that breaks any the least constitution of the Pope. Moreover, he claims authority in three places: heaven, earth, and purgatory; and that is the reason he wears a triple crown; so that by this account and claim, he has more and larger extended authority than God Himself; for such a third place as purgatory is, he does not know of. And what do these things but manifest him, to exalt himself even above God, and all that is worshipped?

3. Antichrist is described to be such a one as should come in "lying signs, and false miracles and wonders," (2 Thes. 2:9). By which, if it were possible, he would deceive the very elect. And that this is verified in the Pope and Popish Church as all men know that have been acquainted with their knavery, deceits, and frauds; so let their Aurea Legenda and book of Torphees testify to the whole world.

4. St. Paul (2 Thes. 2:8) shows by his name, that he speaks of, should be ὁ ἄνομος, that is, *a lawless person*, or one subject to no law; which is also manifestly verified in the Pope; for no laws will hold him, neither Divine nor human: for he claims to be above them all, and to change and alter what he wishes, when he wishes, and to whom he wishes; which the gloss upon the decretals do testify, saying thus of the Pope: *Legi non subjacet ulli*:—that is, He is not subject to any law. What is this else but to be ὁ ἄνομος —a lawless person, even the very same whom St. Paul speaks of?

5. St. John in his Revelation portrays Antichrist

Chapter 5: The False Religion of the Church of Rome

and his seat, by the name of the great whore, with whom have committed fornication the kings of the earth, and the inhabitants of the earth have been drunken with the wine of her fornication. This woman is that great city which had dominion over the kings of the earth, at the time of this revelation, as St. John expressly affirms, (Rev. 17:18). It is well known that there was then no other city which reigned over the kings of the earth, but only Rome; and therefore Rome only is and must necessarily be the seat of Antichrist; for no other can be by this evident and plain description of St. John; for Rome was the only city of the world that reigned over the kings of the earth, the head whereof was then the Emperor, but now the Pope; for the condition of the first beast (namely of the Roman empire civil) is altered and changed into an ecclesiastical and Roman empire.

6. St. John in his Revelation (13:11) saw a beast coming out of the earth, which had two horns like a lamb, and he spoke like a dragon: and then all that is spoken of this beast, fitly and only agrees to that man of Rome the Pope, who though in show he were the lamb; for what is more mild or humble than to call himself the servant of the servants of God? Yet indeed he plays the part of the dragon, or devil, having learned this cunning of Satan; who though he be never so bad a spirit, yet will transform himself into an angel of light, to deceive souls, (2 Cor. 11:14,) as the Apostle shows. "But here is wisdom: (John says in that Revelation): Let him that has understanding count the number of the beast; for it is the number of a man; and his

number is six hundred threescore and six," (verse 18). Now because the number of this wicked beast contains six hundred threescore and six, Irenaeus thinks that this antichristian beast should be λατεῖνος, that is, *a man of Italy*, for the number of the beast is set down in great letters, and this Greek word (*Lateinos*) makes up the just number of six hundred threescore and six, which is the number of the beast's name. If any do think, that though this Revelation were written in Greek, as being the more known and common language, yet that it was uttered to St. John in Hebrew, because the Hebrew tongue is the holy tongue, and that St. John himself was an Hebrew or Jew by nation, and that likewise divers Hebrew words are found in the Revelation, (whose opinion is not unlikely, but very probable,) then let him seek out an Hebrew word, which contains that just number; and herein he need not search far, or to study much upon the matter; for the Hebrew word *Romiith* (that is, *Romanus*, a man of Rome in English) does in those Hebrew letters contain the just number of six hundred threescore and six, which is the number of the name of that antichristian beast: and so by the number of the name to be accounted, either by Greek letters, or by Hebrew letters, it is perfectly agreeing to that man of Rome the Pope. All the marks agreeing to Antichrist (whatsoever they be) are found fully and only accomplished in the Pope; and therefore there is no doubt but he is that notable Antichrist of whom Paul and St. John in his Revelation do testify; and consequently the Church of Rome being not the true Church of Christ, but contrariwise, the visible Church of Antichrist, is justly forsaken, and forever to be forsaken of all Christians, as they tender their salvation in Jesus Christ; to whom only they have betrothed themselves, and to whom they must remain constant for evermore; which God grant us all to do. *Amen.*

CHAPTER 6: Against Schismatics

Against Schism and Schismatical Synagogues

Many there be who, out of a godly and zealous mind, do in good sort seek reformation, and for that Church-government, which Christ Himself has instituted in His Church, whom I neither dare, nor do reprove. Others there be, that seek reformation amiss, with venomous and slanderous tongues, railing and reviling against those which understand it; which things do neither grace themselves, nor yet the cause which they would prefer. Other some there be, who, to make the cause of reformation odious, do say, that it abolishes Her Majesty's supreme government and authority in causes ecclesiastical. I would wish all men to speak the truth, and to seek the preferment of God's truth, in a dutiful, peaceable, and charitable sort. Let the cause be made no worse than it is. For my part, I desire no more than every Christian ought, namely, that the truth of God should carry the preeminence, whatsoever it be. And I would to God that (all malice and contention set apart) all of all parts would grow more charitably affected both in their words, and in their writings one towards another; for so would this controversy sooner come to an end, and the more speedily be decided. Others there be, who for that in so long a time they cannot see their desired discipline and Church-government to be established, run from our Church, and make a schism and separation from us, erecting discipline by their own authority, condemning our Church to be no Church, that they may make their detestable schism the more allowable: these are the Brownists and Barowists, who will not stay the chief magistrate's pleasure for the establishing of it, nor yet allow to us any Church in England, but themselves. But they (for against them I deal) and you must understand, that a Church may be, yes, a true Church may be and is, though it have neither elders, nor deacons, nor discipline in it; for we read, in Acts 2:41–47, of an assembly of people at Jerusalem, that received the Word of God and believed, and which are expressly called a Church, (and who can or dare deny them to be the true Church of God, since the Holy Ghost so testifies of them?) and yet at that time no deacons were chosen, nor consistories of elders erected: for they were not erected till afterward. And therefore a true Church of God may be, though as yet it do not have these: for this desired discipline is not an essential part of the Church; for it resembles the wall of a city, or a hedge or ditch about a vineyard; and it is a city, though the wall be wanting; and it is a vineyard, though the hedge or ditch be wanting, though so much the less fortified I grant. Inasmuch, therefore, as we have the *preaching* of God's *Holy Word*, and the *right administration of the Sacraments*, (which be the essential marks of the true Church), none ought to forsake our Church for any other defect, corruption, or imperfection: for there *may be* corruptions both in doctrine and discipline some, and yet the Church where they be, the *true Church of God*. Admit (if they will) that minsters in the

Church of England be not rightly created and brought into the Church; will they therefore count they be no ministers? By as good an argument they may say, that he that is brought and born into the world, not according to the right course or order of nature, but otherwise, is no man; for the one comes unorderly into the world, as the other does into the Church. I am sure the corrupt ordination of a minister Does not prove him to be no minister; neither does any other corruption in our Church take away the life and being of a Church; for if a man be diseased and full of corruptions, will any man therefore say he is no man? They say we do not only want the right discipline, but we have also put a wrong discipline in the place of it. But what of this? The error then I confess is great, but yet not such as makes a nullity of our Church, so long as it holds Christ Jesus the life and soul of the Church, and is ready to reform her error, whensoever by good proof it shall be manifested to her. In the meantime their argument is nothing worth; for if a man lose a leg or arm, yet none will deny him to be a man for all this blemish or defect; yes, though he put a wooden leg instead of his leg which he alcks, yet he remains a man still, because his principal parts remain. So though we want that discipline, yet we have the principal parts of the Church, namely, the right preaching of the Word of God, and administration of the Sacraments, and therefore a true Church of God undoubtedly, And if we have a true Church, though not a perfect Church, let the Brownists and Barowists consider from where they are fallen; for if the Church of Christ be the body of Christ, as

Chapter 6: Against Schism and Schismatical Synagogues

St. Paul affirms, what do they else, but by their schism, and separation, rent themselves from the body of Christ? and then let them remember whose members they be, until they be reunited. Let them no longer for shame charge our Church with idolatry, except they were better able to prove it, which neither they nor all the world shall do. To say (as they say) that a set form of prayer is used in the Church, and exhibited to God, the prayer being framed according to the rule of God's Word, is idolatry, is detestable: for by as good reason they may condemn all prayer made to God by the preacher or pastor of the congregation; which they will not do; and besides, all the reformed Churches in Christendom have a set form of public prayers for public meetings and congregations.

They say that we observe saints' days, and dedicate Churches to them; but they should show that we do these things in honour of the saints, else have they no reason to charge our Church with idolatry, (as wickedly they do,) for the statute itself expresses, that our Church calls them holy-days, not for the saints' sake, but for the holy exercises used upon them in the public assemblies. Again, true it is, that divers Churches amongst us are called by the names of those saints they are dedicated to: but to say therefore we do dedicate Churches to them, it is very ridiculous: for when we call St. Peter's Church, or St. Paul's Church, it is but to distinguish them from other Churches by their names. In Athens there was a place which bare the name of Mars, and St. Luke calls it "Mars hill," (Acts 17:22); will any man therefore be so foolish or so fond, as to say therefore he committed idolatry? or that therefore he dedicated that place to that heathen god of battle? None I think will be so wicked or absurd.

Moreover, it is true that we observe fasting-days; but in it we observe no Romish fasts, nor place in it the worship of God, nor the remission of our sins, nor the merit of eternal life (as the Papists do). But the politic laws of this land, which appoint that men shall not eat flesh upon certain days, do it in respect of the Commonwealth, as to maintain navigation so much the better, and for spare of the breed of young cattle; appointing moreover a penalty for such as shall take the days to be observed as meritorious Romish fasts.

I therefore wish them to cease their slander against this Church, and to cease their *damnable schism*, and to be reconciled to that Church of ours, from where have they *foolishly* departed; for how imperfect a Church it is, (whose imperfections God cures in His good time,) yet shall they never be able to show otherwise, but that the Church of England is the true Church of God, from which it is utterly unlawful to make a separation.

God forgive us all and reconcile us to Him. Amen.

Other Works Published by Puritan Publications

1. 1647 Westminster Confession of Faith 3rd Edition – KJV Bible
2. A Biblical Response to Superstition, Will-Worship and the Christmas Holiday – by Daniel Cawdrey (1588-1664)
3. A Devotional on Our Savior's Death and Passion by Charles Herle (1598-1659)
4. A Discourse on Church Discipline and Reformation – by Daniel Cawdrey (1588-1664)
5. A Glimpse of God's Glory – Thomas Hodges (1600-1672)
6. A Golden Topaz, or Heart-Jewel, Namely, a Conscience Purified and Pacified by the Blood and Spirit of Christ – by Francis Whiddon (d. 1656) 2nd Ed.
7. A Sermon Against Lukewarmness in Religion – by Henry Wilkinson (1566-1647)
8. A Treatise of the Loves of Christ to His Spouse by Samuel Bolton, D.D. (1606-1654)
9. A Treatise on Divine Contentment – by Simeon Ashe (d. 1662)
10. A Vindication of the Keys of the Kingdom of Heaven into the Hands of the Right Owners – by Daniel Cawdrey (1588-1664)
11. Armilla Catechetica, or a Chain of Theological Principles – by John Arrowsmith (1602-1659)
12. Attending the Lord's Table – by Henry Tozer (1602-1650)
13. Christ Inviting Sinners to Come to Him for Rest – by Jeremiah Burroughs (1599-1646)
14. Christ the Settlement in Unsettled Times – Jeremiah Whitaker (1599–1654)
15. Ezra's Covenant Renewal and the Pursuit of a Lasting Reformation - by Josiah Shute (1588-1643)
16. Family Reformation Promoted, and Other Works – by

Daniel Cawdrey (1588-1664)
17. God is Our Refuge and Our Strength by George Gipps (n.d.)
18. God Paying Every Man His Due – Francis Woodcock (1614-1649)
19. God With Us, and Other Works – by John Strickland (1601-1670)
20. God, the Best Acquaintance of Christians – by Matthew Newcomen (1610–1669)
21. God's Voice from His Throne of Glory – by John Carter (d. 1655)
22. Gospel Peace, Or Four Useful Discourses – by Jeremiah Burroughs (1599-1646)
23. Gospel Worship, or, The Right Manner of Sanctifying the name of God in General, in Hearing the Word, Receiving the Lord's Supper, and Prayer by Jeremiah Burroughs (1599-1646)
24. Gradual Reformation Intolerable – by C. Matthew McMahon and Anthony Burgess (1600-1663)
25. Halting Stigmatized – by Arthur Sallaway (b. 1606)
26. How to Serve God in Private and Public Worship – by John Jackson (1600-1648)
27. Independency A Great Schism – by Daniel Cawdrey (1588-1664)
28. Jacob's Seed and David's Delight – by Jeremiah Burroughs (1599-1646)
29. Jesus Christ God's Shepherd – by William Strong (d. 1654)
30. Making Religion One's Business – by Herbert Palmer (1601-1647)
31. Presumptive Regeneration, or, the Baptismal Regeneration of Elect Infants – by Cornelius Burges (1589-1665)
32. Primitive Baptism and Therein Infant's and Parent's Rights by Matthew Sylvester (1636–1708)
33. Real Thankfulness – by Simeon Ashe (d. 1662)
34. Reasonable Christianity – by Henry Hammond (1605-1660)

35. Reformation and Desolation – by Stephen Marshall (1594–1655)
36. Regeneration and the New Birth – by Isaac Ambrose (1604–1663)
37. Repentance and Fasting – by Peter Du Moulin (1601-1684) and Henry Wilkinson (1566-1647)
38. Rules for Our Walking With God – by Jeremiah Burroughs (1599-1646)
39. Salvation in a Mystery – by John Bond (1612-1676)
40. Scripture's Self Evidence – by Thomas Ford (1598–1674)
41. Selected Works of Peter Sterry – by Peter Sterry (1613–1672)
42. Sermons, Prayers, and Pulpit Addresses – Alexander Henderson (1583-1646)
43. Singing of Psalms the Duty of Christians – by Thomas Ford (1598–1674)
44. Spots of the Godly and of the Wicked – by Jeremiah Burroughs (1599-1646)
45. The All-Seeing Unseen Eye of God and Other Sermons – by Matthew Newcomen (1610–1669)
46. The Art of Divine Meditation by Edmund Calamy (1600-1666)
47. The Art of Happiness – by Francis Rous (1579–1659)
48. The Certainty of Heavenly and the Uncertainty of Earthly Treasures – by William Strong (d. 1654)
49. The Christian's Duty Towards Reformation – by Thomas Ford (1598–1674)
50. The Church's Need of Jesus Christ – by Thomas Valentine (1586-1665)
51. The Comfort of Christ to Weak Believers – by John Durant (1620-1686)
52. The Covenant of Life Opened – by Samuel Rutherford (1600-1661)
53. The Covenant of Works and the Covenant of Grace – by Edmund Calamy (1600-1666)
54. The Covenant-Avenging Sword Brandished – by John

Arrowsmith (1602-1659)
55. The Difficulties of and Encouragements to a Reformation – Anthony Burgess (1600-1663) 2nd Ed.
56. The Doctrine of Man's Future Eternity – by John Jackson (1600-1648)
57. The Efficiency of God's Grace in Bringing Gain-Saying Sinners to Christ – by Simeon Ashe (d. 1662)
58. The Eternity and Certainty of Hell's Torments – by William Strong (d. 1654)
59. The Excellency of Holy Courage in Evil Times – by Jeremiah Burroughs (1599-1646)
60. The Excellent Name of God - by Jeremiah Burroughs (1599-1646)
61. The Fall of Adam and Other Works – by John Greene (d. 1660)
62. The Glorious Name of God the Lord of Hosts by Jeremiah Burroughs (1599-1646)
63. The Glory and Beauty of God's Portion and Other Sermons – by Gaspar Hickes, (d. 1677)
64. The Godly Man's Ark – by Edmund Calamy (1600-1666)
65. The Growth and Spreading of Heresy – by Thomas Hodges (1600-1672)
66. The Guard of the Tree of Life, a Discourse on the Sacraments – by Samuel Bolton (1606-1654)
67. The Light of Faith and Way of Holiness – by Richard Byfield (1598–1664)
68. The Manifold Wisdom of God Seen in Covenant Theology – by George Walker (1581-1651)
69. The Nature, Danger and Cure of Temptation by Richard Capel (1586–1656)
70. The Necessity, Dignity and Duty of Gospel Ministers – by Thomas Hodges (1600-1672)
71. The Rock of Israel and Other Sermons – by Edmund Staunton (1600-1671)
72. The Saint's Communion with God – by William Strong,

A.M. (d. 1654)
73. The Saint's Inheritance and the Worldling's Portion – by Jeremiah Burroughs (1599-1646)
74. The Saint's Will Judge the World, and Other Sermons – by Daniel Cawdrey (1588-1664)
75. The Sermons of William Spurstowe (1605-1666)
76. The Soul's Porter, or a Treatise on the Fear of God – by William Price (1597-1646)
77. The Spiritual Chemyst, or Divine Meditations on Several Subjects – by William Spurstowe (1605-1666)
78. The Sweetness of Divine Meditation by William Bridge (1600-1670)
79. The Trial of a Christian's Sincere Love to Christ – by William Pinke (1599–1629)
80. The Wells of Salvation Opened – by William Spurstowe (1605-1666)
81. The Works of Richard Greenham Volume 1 – by Richard Greenham (1531-1594)
82. The Worthy Churchman, or the Faithful Minister of Jesus Christ – by John Jackson (1600-1648)
83. The Zealous Christian – by Simeon Ashe (d. 1662)
84. Truth, the Great Business of Our Times – by John Maynard (1600-1665)
85. Zeal for God's House Quickened – by Oliver Bowles B.D. (1574-1664?)
86. Zion's Joy – Jeremiah Burroughs (1599-1646)